WITHDRAWN

How to Write and Prepare Training Materials

)NDON BOROUGH OF BROMLEY

The Kogan Page Practical Trainer Series

Series Editor: Roger Buckley

PRACTICAL TRAINER SERIES

KOGAN PAGE

How to Write and Prepare Training Materials

NANCY STIMSON

KOGAN PAGE
Published in association with the
Institute of Training and Development

To my long-suffering family

First published in 1991

Kogan Page Limited
120 Pentonville Road
London N1 9JN

© Nancy Stimson, 1991

British Library Cataloguing in Publication Data

A CIP record for this book is available from the British Library.

ISBN 07494 0442 6

Typeset by Saxon Printing Ltd, Derby
Printed and bound in Great Britain by Biddles Ltd, Guildford

Contents

LIST OF FIGURES

Series Editor's Foreword

Organizations get things done when people do their jobs effectively. To make this happen they need to be well trained. A number of people are likely to be involved in this training by identifying the needs of the organization and of the individual, by selecting or designing appropriate training to meet those needs, by delivering it and by assessing how effective it was. It is not only 'professional' or full-time trainers who are involved in this process: personnel managers, line managers, supervisors and job holders are all likely to have a part to play.

This series has been written for all those who get involved with training in some way or another, whether they are senior personnel managers trying to link the goals of the organization with training needs or job holders who have been given responsibility for training newcomers. Therefore, the series is essentially a practical one which focuses on specific aspects of the training function. This is not to say that the theoretical underpinnings of the practical aspects of training are unimportant. Anyone seriously interested in training is strongly encouraged to look beyond 'what to do' and 'how to do it' and to delve into the areas of why things are done in a particular way.

The authors have been selected because they have considerable practical experience. All have shared, at some time, the same difficulties, frustrations and satisfactions of being involved in training and are now in a position to share with others some helpful and practical guidelines.

All trainers would agree that they have to be good communicators. To many of us this means standing up and teaching a group of trainees or tutoring someone on a one-to-one basis. However, trainers spend a large proportion of their time in preparing written material.

In this book, Nancy Stimson provides practical guidelines on the structure, style and grammar of a range of documents that trainers have to produce. These include job descriptions, lesson notes, visual aids, handouts and the like. It is vital that these are produced to a high standard not only for the purposes of effective communication but because they reflect the professionalism and the credibility of the trainer.

ROGER BUCKLEY

Acknowledgements

I would like to thank Her Majesty's Stationery Office for permission to reproduce Winston Churchill's minute on brevity, and the Training and Development Lead Body for permission to quote passages from the National Standards for Training and Development.

I would also like to thank my editors, Dolores Black and Roger Buckley, for their help and advice, and my 'target reader', Pella Munday.

Introduction

How to Write Everything Trainers Write

As a trainer you probably think of yourself as someone who speaks to people – large seminar audiences, small workshop groups, individual managers and employees. But trainers are not just speakers, they are prolific writers too. In achieving the trainer's objective, helping someone to learn something, there are several typical stages:

- Identifying what should be done (and recording this in job descriptions, job aids, procedures manuals, etc).
- Identifying what is being done, and the resulting gap. (This is often recorded in performance appraisal or other reports.)
- Proposing how to resolve the gap (probably in a memo, report or other written form).
- Delivering training inputs (to the accompaniment of course notes, visuals, handouts, exercises, self-learning texts etc).
- Following-up after the training (with doubtless more memos or reports).

All these pieces of writing are 'training materials' in the truest sense of the words. Helping both the novice and experienced trainer write and prepare them is what this book is about.

Trainers have special needs as writers. As we have seen, their output is considerable; they write many different kinds of documents; these go to many different readers. And, to make matters worse, trainers are also expected to be 'expert' in this as in many other fields – they may even have to run 'Writing Skills' courses. It is expecting a lot from professionals whose own basic training usually concentrates on speaking skills.

National competency standards for trainers do acknowledge the importance of writing, stressing that written materials should be 'accurate and in a style and format appropriate to the needs and capabilities of the audience'. But even in this quotation from the UK *National Standards for Training and Development*, the word 'audience' reveals the bias towards face-to-face communication.

This book is an attempt to adjust the balance. It is a three-part writing resource for trainers.

Part 1 provides a brief refresher on writing principles. It examines how you can make life easy for your reader (and therefore improve your chances of achieving your objectives) by planning your writing, choosing your words carefully, presenting the material attractively, and editing it to make sure it says and does what you want. There are a number of exercises to help you hone your skills, as well as checklists to act as memory-joggers.

Part 2 considers all the various 'materials' trainers may write:

– Job descriptions	– Course visuals
– Performance standards	– Course handouts
– Performance objectives	– Course exercises.
– Procedures	– Self-learning texts
– Job aids	– Reports
– Manuals	– Letters
– Forms	– Memos
– Questionnaires	– Minutes of meetings
– Course notes	

The chapters in Part 2 give tips on how to handle these writing tasks, standard formats and examples. Use them to pick up practical hints, ideas and suggestions.

Part 3 is for reference, and also for interest. It is a collection of chapters on various associated topics: source materials, copyright, grammar, punctuation, spelling, tables and charts, and using technology. Dip into the chapters as you need them.

In a sense, Part 1, together with the add-ons in Part 3, form a foundation of writing skill and knowledge which can then be applied to all the different documents that trainers write.

Writing can be a chore or it can be a delight. Enjoy your writing, and this book!

Part 1 Writing Basics

1 Writing To Be Read

<table>
<tr><td>▷</td><td align="center">SUMMARY</td><td>◁</td></tr>
</table>

Writers need to be read, and therefore to make their writing attractive to readers by focusing from the reader's point of view. This is a chapter of questions, Kipling's 'six faithful serving men'. Before writing, ask yourself:

- **Why** are you writing? What objective do you want your reader to achieve?
- **Who** is your reader? What do you know about him/her/them? Do multiple readers have conflicting needs?
- **How** do you want to write? What format and tone?
- **When** do you write best? How can you meet your deadline?
- **Where** do you write best?
- **What** should you include? How should you structure your material?

Writers Need to be Read

Do you read everything that piles up in your in-tray? Do all your intended readers read everything you have written? The amount of paper going straight from in-tray to wastepaper bin represents a horrific cost, in money terms, in environmental terms, and in wasted writer-hours.

Writers need to be read. And, just as important, they need to be understood correctly. For the reality of your communication, of course, lies not in what you wanted to write, or even what you did write, but in what your reader understood.

Let us see what, from a reader's point of view, are the barriers to reading and understanding:

- Too much else to do.
- The document seems irrelevant to his or her needs.
- The length (or even weight!) of the document. We all tend to deal with short matters first, and push the long reports to the bottom of the pile.
- It is visually unattractive, with long paragraphs, small margins and no headings.
- The structure is poor, with no logical links between points.
- The language is difficult to understand, with long words and sentences, jargon and technical terms.

As a writer you can and must break down these barriers. You can even influence your intended reader's workload by considering, before you pick up your pen: 'Should I write at all? Why?' There are good reasons for writing:

- To establish a permanent record.
- To make the message more formal.
- To convey the same message to many people.
- It can be comparatively cheap, at least in direct costs.
- Delivery and response may be reasonably rapid (using fax, telex or electronic mail) or more delayed (postal systems), whichever you want.

But in many cases, a telephone call or quick face-to-face chat are more effective. If so, don't write; talk.

Readers and Objectives

Once you have decided that you *should* be writing, your next question is not 'To whom should I write?' but '*Who needs to read this?*' The difference is more than just one of phraseology – it is one of approach, of putting your reader first and seeing through his or her eyes rather than your own, probably the single golden rule which will make any communication more effective.

Effectiveness, achieving your objective, is after all the sole reason for communicating. You do need to have the objective clear in your mind, of course. Think back to your last piece of writing. What was your objective? When asked this question, even experienced trainers, accustomed to expressing training objectives in terms of trainees' desired behaviour, are liable to answer: 'I wanted to say ...' But behavioural objectives are just as important for writing as for training courses. Stating what you 'want the reader to do ...' is the first step to having that happen.

As with training objectives, the key to formulating behavioural objectives for your writing lies in making your reader the subject of the sentence, and then using an 'action verb'. So start your objectives with the formula: **After reading this, my reader will ...** and continue with an 'action verb', not the vague **know, understand, appreciate** which so easily spring to mind, but the specific **decide, carry out, complete, remember**.

For example, the objectives of a joining letter to managers nominated to attend a presentation skills course could be:

Readers (managers nominated to attend the presentation skills course) will:

- **Attend the course.**
- **Want to attend the course.**
- **Know when and where to go, and what to bring with them.**
- **Identify their personal needs for the course.**
- **Prepare themselves for the course.**
- **Know what to expect from the course.**
- **Be prepared to admit and address their fears and weaknesses.**
- **Let the organizers know if they cannot attend the course.**

The behavioural nature of the objective may be obvious ('attend the course') or less so ('*want* to attend the course', and show this in behaviour, however subtly). As a bottom line objective, you should always want all your readers to remember what you have written or, at least, *that* you have written something on the subject. If even that is not really necessary for some readers (or more likely non-readers), remove them from your distribution list. Their in-trays will be grateful!

Having a single reader simplifies your job as writer; it is, however, comparatively rare. Even a letter or memo addressed to one person may, predictably, be shown to others.

Whether you have one reader or several, the more you know about them, the better. First of all, their names. 'Dear Sir or Madam' letters should be avoided wherever possible.

Then consider:

- How well do they understand your language (both the English language and your technical jargon)?
- How much do they know about the subject?
- What are their concerns and prejudices likely to be?

   – What authority do they have?
   – What could prevent them achieving your objectives?

If you cannot answer these questions, a little initial research will save a lot of later frustration.

Sometimes, if you have multiple readers, their needs may conflict. You may be able to accommodate this in your writing, for instance, by putting background details, needed by only *some* readers of a report, in an appendix. You may concentrate on meeting the needs of your most important reader, not necessarily in status terms, but the person who will achieve your objective. You may write different documents – the full report for the person who needs to know all the details, and a summary, or a note explaining what the report covers and where it is filed, for the person who only needs to know that it has been written. Or you may just have to live with the conflict (for example, where one trainee may need the course joining letter to stimulate his excitement and another to reassure his fears) and mitigate the effects by talking to the people concerned.

Planning

All this is part of your initial planning. It answers Kipling's '**why**' and '**who**' questions. He had four others:

How? What format you should choose, eg letter, memo, report, is also important. Part 2 of this book gives tips on how to handle the different writing tasks you may need to perform. 'How' should also cover the tone you want to convey – formal or friendly, rational or inspirational, decisive or questioning.

When? If you have a deadline, meet it. If you do not have a deadline, set yourself one and meet it. To see if the deadline is realistic, work backwards from it, and judge how long you should allow for revision, typing, writing, planning and research. Do you have enough time? If not, can you change your deadline? If not, what can you reduce? Maybe someone else can do part of your research; maybe you will have to limit the scope of what you cover. But, for your reader's sake (and therefore your own), meet your deadline.

Also consider the time of day when you work best. Some of us are larks, wide awake and fully functioning in the early morning; others are owls, animated in the evening. Whichever you are, choose if you can that time for writing.

Where? Balance the peacefulness of writing at home, without the distractions of telephone and interruptions, with the convenience of having all your information available at the office. An empty training room, or even someone else's office, could prove the ideal solution. And, wherever you write, set up your environment to make it as easy as possible – comfortable chair, good lighting, telephone off-the-hook, reference materials to hand.

Structure

The last question is '**what?**' What material, what points do you include? And in what order?

First, decide what your main point is and at what stage you want to make it. It often seems logical to leave it until the end, and build up to it with supporting data. But your reader may not read to the end. Try and make your main point as early as you can, maybe even in the first paragraph of a memo or letter, or at the beginning of the summary of a report.

Then consider the rest of your content from the reader's position. For each item, ask yourself, 'Does my reader need to know this? Why?' The order of your material, too, should depend on the reader and your objective.

There are various techniques to help you structure your writing. The simplest is merely to list your points and juggle them around, either by numbering your list or, physically, by writing each point on adhesive 'stickers'. These points then form separate sections or paragraphs.

Other structuring techniques use visual effects (placing, colour, size, pictures) to help you recognise links between points. Decision trees, flowcharts and 'mind maps' are examples of these.

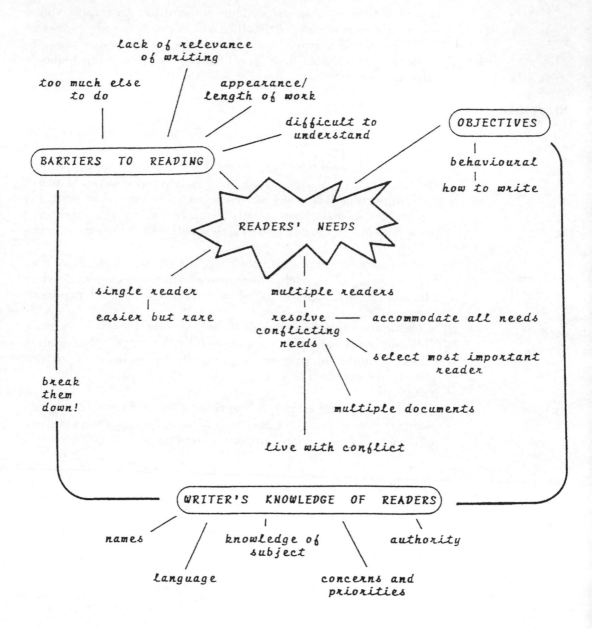

Figure 1.1 *Mind map*

CHECKLIST

WRITING TO BE READ

Before starting to write, do you consider:	OK	Could be better	Should be better
• Whether you should write at all?	—	—	—
• Who your reader is?	—	—	—
• Whether you know enough about your reader?	—	—	—
• What your objective is, in behavioural terms?	—	—	—
• What your reader's needs are?	—	—	—
• How to resolve the conflicting needs of multiple readers?	—	—	—
• What format you want to use?	—	—	—
• What tone you want to use?	—	—	—
• How to meet your deadline?	—	—	—
• When you write best?	—	—	—
• Where you write best?	—	—	—
• What your main point is, and where you will place it?	—	—	—
• What other points you will include?	—	—	—
• How you will structure them?	—	—	—

2 Choosing Your Words

▷ SUMMARY ◁

- Despite all your planning, sometimes the words just will not come. Tactics for overcoming writer's block include: postponement; subdividing the writing task; starting in the middle or at the end; systematically expanding 'brainstormed' ideas; dictating; or typing.
- Tools to help you find the right word include dictionaries and *Roget's Thesaurus*. Misuse of words leads to confusion.
- The best writing is composed of short, simple, familiar words in short, simple sentences (KISS). Some useful guidelines are:

  - Eliminate redundancies.
  - Avoid jargon.
  - Prefer the positive to the negative.
  - Prefer concrete to abstract nouns.
  - Prefer verbs to nouns.
  - Prefer active to passive verb forms.
  - Use the first and second person pronouns ('I' and 'you').
  - Use non-sexist language.

- The complexity of a piece of writing may be measured by Robert Gunning's FOG Index, which is based on word and sentence length.

Writer's Block

Blank mind and blank paper – a state familiar to all writers, because however well you have planned your writing, sometimes those critical first words just will not come.

Probably the best way of handling this situation is, if possible, to postpone writing – sleep on it, take a walk round the block, or even take a bath. It was not through chance that Archimedes cried 'Eureka' in his bath: immersion in water produces physical and mental relaxation, which allows the super-efficient unconscious mind to resolve any outstanding problems.

Other tactics, more acceptable in the office, include subdividing the writing task, and starting in the middle or at the end – anywhere apart from the blocked beginning. Another approach is to 'brainstorm'. Give yourself a time limit (say 5–10 minutes) and write down as many phrases, thoughts, images as you can think of. Do not try to revise or polish these: you are aiming for quantity, not quality. Having got some material, you can then build systematically on this and on the plan you have already produced, expanding points, linking up your 'brainstormed' words and ideas, and adding examples.

If all else fails, throw away the pen and paper. Some people find it less off-putting to type directly onto a typewriter or word processor screen. Others prefer to talk, dictating to a tape recorder or simply explaining the material to a friend.

Finding the 'Right' Word

Once you have got started, don't stop to hunt down an elusive term. First drafts are not meant to be perfect. If you are stuck on a word, leave a gap or put down an approximation, and go on. When you come to revise your draft later on, you may find the exact word leaps out at you. If not, tools such as dictionaries, synonym dictionaries (as used by crossword puzzle addicts), or *Roget's Thesaurus* can be a great help.

They are also useful for expanding your vocabulary (it is estimated that the vocabulary of English-speaking adults may vary from 12,000 to 30,000 words), and browsing in dictionaries can bring surprising revelations about words you thought you understood.

Misunderstood and misused words can be highly dangerous. If I *realize* that I do not understand the word 'continually' which you have included in safety instructions, I can ask you to explain it. But if I think it means 'constantly' or 'without stopping', and you (correctly) intend it to mean 'repeatedly', we have a problem. **Evacuate the building when the fire alarm sounds continually** is a recipe for chaos and disaster.

Figure 2.1 *What do they mean?*

Many words are commonly misused, sometimes even changing the meaning of the sentence completely. Here are some pairs of words which are often confused. What do they mean?

1 AFFECT / EFFECT
2 ALTERNATE / ALTERNATIVE
3 BI- / SEMI-
4 COMPLEMENT / COMPLIMENT
5 IE / EG

6 DISINTERESTED / UNINTERESTED
7 IMPLY / INFER
8 PRINCIPAL / PRINCIPLE
9 PRACTISE / PRACTICE
10 LIE / LAY

1 AFFECT is a verb meaning 'have an effect on'. EFFECT is both a noun meaning 'result' and a verb meaning 'cause' or 'bring about':

The budget limitations affected all departments. The main effect was a 10 per cent salary cut for all staff, which effected a dramatic increase in staff turnover.

2 ALTERNATE is both a verb meaning to 'take it in turn' and an adjective meaning 'every other'. ALTERNATIVE is normally a noun meaning 'choice'. It is also used as an adjective meaning 'other', sometimes creating an unnecessary repetition. (There is no difference between 'The alternative is...' and 'The alternative option is ... '):

Until an alternative solution is found, Ann and John will carry out the receptionist's duties on alternate days.
Until another alternative is found, Ann and John will alternate as receptionist.

3 BI- means 'every two' (days, weeks, months etc). SEMI- means 'half':
Semi-mensual meetings are held bi-weekly.
(However 'biannual' means 'twice a year' or 'half-yearly'; 'biennial' means 'every two years'.)

4 COMPLEMENT is a noun or verb that refers to 'making something complete'. COMPLIMENT is a noun or verb meaning 'praise':

Frequent compliments to employees for good work will complement a supervisor's other efforts to improve performance.

5 IE is an abbreviation meaning 'that is'. EG is an abbreviation meaning 'for example':

> **The role of the trainer, ie someone who trains others as a part of his or her job, may be performed by many different people, eg managers, supervisors, colleagues.**
>
> 6 DISINTERESTED means 'without ulterior motive'. UNINTERESTED means 'bored' or 'unreceptive':
>
> **Although it was a disinterested piece of advice, the employee remained uninterested.**
>
> 7 IMPLY means 'suggest'. INFER means 'deduce':
>
> **The consultant implied that we should first tackle our technical training deficiencies; however, we inferred from our internal surveys that poor communication was a greater problem.**
>
> 8 PRINCIPAL is an adjective meaning 'chief' or 'most important'. It is also a noun meaning the 'principal person'. PRINCIPLE is a noun meaning 'fundamental rule':
>
> **The school principal's principal task that day was to work out budgetary control principles.**
>
> 9 PRACTISE is a verb and PRACTICE is a noun (except in America where PRACTICE is both verb and noun – see Chapter 18).
>
> **The girl did her piano practice although she did not enjoy practising.**
>
> 10 LIE is an intransitive verb meaning 'assume a lying position'. LAY, as a verb, has various meanings, but the confusion with LIE arises because LAY is a transitive verb meaning 'to place in a lying position.' It is also the past tense of LIE.
>
> **'I will lay the papers straight so that they lie tidily on the desk,' he said. He then lay down to rest.**

KISS

The best way to avoid misunderstandings is to choose your words carefully. KISS stands for:

KEEP
IT
SHORT and
SIMPLE.

Polysyllables are cumbersome – aren't they?
People sometimes think, however, that long words and sentences look more impressive and professional than short ones. Let Churchill, the ultimate impressive, professional communicator, rebut that.

To do our work, we all have to read a mass of papers. Nearly all of them are far too long. This wastes time, while energy has to be spent in looking for the essential points.

I ask my colleagues and their staffs to see to it that their reports are shorter.

(i)   The aim should be reports which set out the main points in a series of short crisp paragraphs.

(ii) If a report relies on a detailed analysis of some complicated factors, or on statistics, these should be set out in an appendix.

(iii) Often the occasion is best met by submitting not a full-dress report, but an aide-memoire consisting of headings only, which can be expanded orally if needed.

(iv) Let us have an end of such phrases as these:

'It is also of importance to bear in mind the following considerations ... ' or 'Consideration should be given to the possibility of carrying into effect ... '

Most of these woolly phrases are mere padding, which can be left out altogether, or replaced by a single word. Let us not shrink from using the short, expressive phrase, even if it is conversational.

Reports drawn up on the lines I propose may at first seem rough as compared with the flat surface of officialese jargon, but the saving in time will be great, while the discipline of setting out the real points concisely will prove an aid to clearer thinking.

10 Downing Street
9th August 1940.   WSC.

Figure 2.2   *It was ever thus...*

The Plain English Campaign originated to rid official language of its 'gobbledegook', and public documents certainly have improved. For instance,the latest instructions for completing income tax forms are models of simplicity and clarity, a far cry from those of earlier years.

National newspapers, too, have followed suit and run competitions to expose particularly tortuous examples of commercialese. Some of the competitions even invite readers to rewrite these passages in comprehensible English. It is surprising how easy it can be to eliminate redundancies and avoid long, convoluted words and sentences.

Short, simple words are easy both to write and understand.

Don't write this —	But this —
Along the lines of ...	Like
In the majority of instances ...	Usually
Give consideration to ...	Consider
A large number of ...	Many
In spite of the fact that ...	Although
During the period that ...	While
Rectangular in shape ...	Rectangular
The month of December ...	December
In order to ...	To
Recur again ...	Recur
Entirely completed ...	Completed
In the not too distant future ...	Soon
On the part of ...	By
It would seem reasonable to believe ...	I believe
The data appears to indicate ...	I think

Figure 2.3 *KISS words*

Jargon

Everyone knows that jargon is bad – but it is not, necessarily. Using your readers' jargon is excellent for making them feel you understand their needs, and goes a long way to persuading them to accept your suggestions.

Jargon is merely technical terminology. It enables you to communicate technical information shortly and precisely, *provided your reader understands it.* Jargon which is not understood, however, should be avoided; it leaves your reader confused, irritated and often suspicious of your motives. Even worse is jargon which can be misunderstood, for instance words used in a technical sense which have a slightly different every-day meaning.

Much of the trainer's jargon falls into this category eg 'facilitate', 'reinforcement', 'feedback', 'model', 'counselling', even 'needs' and 'learning'. Beware:

Reinforcement of the learning is facilitated by the use of feedback, models, and needs-based counselling!

Positives and Negatives

As trainers, we are all very much accustomed to phrasing negative comments positively, sometimes too much so. As one never-to-be-forgotten student once said to me, 'Please don't keep saying "That's interesting" when you mean "That's wrong"!' Nevertheless positive talking and writing does work. You are much likelier to discover 'creative' solutions, if you refer to 'challenges' and 'opportunities' than if you talk about 'problems'.

Positive forms of speech are also much easier to understand and more persuasive than negative ones.

Contrast: **Please call me if ...** and **Please do not hesitate to call me if ...** Contrast: **I will return your call at once,** and **I will not delay in returning your call.**

Double and triple negatives can totally obscure your meaning. **There is no reason to doubt that his request will not be granted** – well, will it be granted or not?

Concrete and Abstract Nouns

Another concept familiar to trainers is the power of the concrete, visual image. I am certainly well aware of it – why, then, have I just, automatically, written 'concept', 'power' and 'image', instead of: **Trainers also know how well people remember pictures?**

The principal reason is that we tend to *think* in abstractions, and then naturally write down our thoughts in the same words. The trouble is that abstractions, being 'thinking' words, are more likely to have subtly different meanings for different people. For instance, you may have thought I meant: **Trainers also know how easily pictures influence people.** In fact, I may not even be quite sure of my own meaning. Abstractions are such convenient 'labels' for thoughts, that we often attach them too quickly, and this actually stops us from fully understanding and developing our own thoughts.

Expressing abstract ideas in concrete words is a knack which improves with practice. Here are a few examples of overworked abstractions together with more precise and concrete substitutes:

- facilities:
  not **refreshment facilities** but **coffee machine**.
- communication:
  not **written communication** but **report**.
- procedures:
  not **financial recording procedures** but **bookkeeping.**
- condition:
  not **error condition** but **mistake.**
- arrangements:
  not **lunch arrangements** but **sandwiches.**

– situation:
not **unfavourable meteorological situation** but **rain.**

Look back on a few of your recent reports and create your own blacklist of the abstractions you favour.

Verbs and Nouns

Another way of reducing abstractions and making your writing more vivid is to carry the sense of your phrase in the verb rather than in nouns. For example:

> **help,** not **be of assistance.**
> **tell,** not **give information.**
> **change,** not **carry out alterations.**

Active and Passive Verbs

This is probably the easiest and most effective 'quick fix' of all for making your writing strong and persuasive. Managers, including training managers, traditionally write reports in the passive voice:

An investigation of needs was performed and it was then decided that a two-day training course would be prepared and run, within which the issue of improving managers' negotiation skills would be addressed.

You could equally well write:

I investigated the negotiation skill needs of managers, and will prepare and run a two-day training course to meet those needs.

The second passage in fact gives more information than the first, specifying who has done or will do what. That may be one of the reasons for the popularity of the passive – writers can hide behind the welter of words, without actually committing themselves personally to doing anything. Of course, that is precisely the impression that comes across to the reader ...

'I' and 'You'

Using the active voice forces use of the pronokns 'I', 'you', 'we', 'they', etc. (Watch 'we' and 'they' which, again, are good camouflage words.) It

It may be appropriate, in a progress report, to use 'I' repeatedly. In a letter or memo intended to persuade, sell or influence, however, the most valuable pronoun is 'you'.

You explained your managers' problems with negotiating. I will prepare and run a two-day training course to meet your needs is subtly different from the earlier version above.

'He' and 'She'

'You' also gets round some of the problems of non-sexist language. 'He or she', 's/he', 'he/she' all read awkwardly and are best avoided if possible. You can sometimes use the plural 'they'; you can sometimes recast the sentence completely; but watch the dangers of abstractions and passive verbs. Here are some variations:

- **A trainer may feel that he needs to impress his participants.**
- **A trainer may feel that [he or she] / [s/he] / [he/she] needs to impress [his or her] / [his/her] participants.**
- **Trainers may feel that they need to impress their participants.**
- **You, as a trainer, may feel you need to impress your participants.**
- **A trainer may consider impressing participants important.**

Make life easy for your readers. Which version do you prefer?

1 Computer equipment is available to us through a variety of hardware manufacturer supply outlets. (14 words)

or

We have several computer suppliers. (5 words)

2 Due consideration has been given to the question of the comparative desirability of A over B, concluding that this should be resolved on a direct cost basis. (27 words)

or

We should choose the cheaper of A or B. (9 words)

3 Communication difficulties are being experienced in interface situations between the Marketing and Accounts functions. (14 words)

or

Marketing and Accounts do not talk to each other. (9 words)

4 It is felt by the task force that, as a first step, a proper analysis of the disciplinary procedures should be conducted. (22 words)

or

The task force want to analyse disciplinary procedures first. (9 words)

5 The impossibility of the proposition is evident. (7 words)
or
It is impossible. (3 words)
6 The nature of the location is such as to produce an atmosphere of relaxation and tranquillity. (16 words)
or
It is a peaceful place. (5 words)

Figure 2.4 *KISS sentences*

FOG Index

Having KISSed your language, you may want to see how successful you were. A handy tip is to try reading your draft aloud. Does it 'sound wrong' – is your tongue tripping over awkward words; do you run out of breath half-way through the sentence? Then run a more systematic test.

Robert Gunning's FOG Index is a convenient way of checking how simple your writing is. It is based on word and sentence length, and includes a factor to make it represent the approximate years of schooling needed to understand the language easily. The lower the FOG Index, the simpler the passage. Most classic writing has a low FOG Index (7 or 8); much business writing scores 17+. A good target is 12.

To calculate your FOG Index, take a 100-word sample and identify the average number of words per sentence (ending in a full stop or a colon or semi-colon.) Count also the number of polysyllables (words with three or more syllables) in the 100 words, excluding capitalized words and verb forms where the third syllable is -ing, -es, or -ed, eg carrying, attaches, committed.

Add the average sentence length to the number of polysyllables and multiply by 0·4.

As an example, the FOG Index of Churchill's memo which I quoted earlier is calculated as follows:

Average sentence length – 18 words
Polysyllables – 21 in whole memo, ie 9 per 100 words
$(18 + 9) \times 0{\cdot}4 =$ a FOG Index of 11, which means that most school-leavers should be able to understand it.

CHECKLIST

CHOOSING YOUR WORDS

Do you:	OK	Could be better	Should be better
• **Get the words flowing by**			
– doing something else?	—	—	—
– subdividing the writing task?	—	—	—
– starting at the middle/end?	—	—	—
– 'brainstorming' ideas?	—	—	—
– dictating?	—	—	—
– typing?	—	—	—
• **Use dictionaries to**			
– check your meaning?	—	—	—
– browse through?	—	—	—
• **Remember KISS and**			
– eliminate redundancies?	—	—	—
– beware of jargon?	—	—	—
– use positive, not negative, phrases?	—	—	—
– use concrete, not abstract, nouns?	—	—	—
– use verbs, not nouns?	—	—	—
– use active, not passive, verbs?	—	—	—
– use 'I' and 'you'?	—	—	—
– use non-sexist language?	—	—	—
– read your draft aloud?	—	—	—
– apply the FOG Index?	—	—	—

3 Presenting Your Material

▷ SUMMARY ◁

Layout is your responsibility as a writer; it is also your opportunity, as presentation makes an immense difference to how readable and persuasive your writing is. Points to consider are:

- White space
- Paragraphs
- Headings
- Numbering systems and lists

- Emphasis
- Presenting numerical information
- Using pictures

How Much Does Presentation Matter?

It is a cliché of modern marketing that an article can, and even should cost many times more to package than to produce. Appearance may not be all, but it certainly makes a great difference, and one that can profitably be measured in increased sales. In another context, politicians, too, play the 'image' game, and research into interviewing practices has similarly shown that many interview decisions are heavily influenced by first impressions.

The same is true with written material. Professional-looking presentation goes a long way to persuading your reader of your professionalism. Layout which is easy to look at encourages your reader to look and read.

How much consideration do *you* give to the appearance of your material? Leaving layout to the typist, or a company 'house style', is to abandon your responsibility and your opportunity.

White Space

Probably the most influential factor in capturing and keeping your reader's attention, is what you don't write – the white space surrounding your words. A perennial advertising favourite, *white space works.*
Ways of including white space are:

- Gaps between letters (eg l e t t e r s).
- Gaps between words.
- Gaps between lines and paragraphs.
- Length of paragraphs.
- Gaps at the top and bottom of the page.
- Margin widths.
- Indentation.
- Centring text.

These spacing possibilities can easily be controlled, both with word processors and ordinary typewriters.

Paragraphs

Paragraphing, of course, does more than just increase white space. It should not be a matter of chance or whim, as good paragraphing can make your material much easier for your reader to follow. There are two straightforward guidelines:

1 Paragraph length.
   Each paragraph should cover a single main issue. An average of about six to eight lines per paragraph is about right for most business writing. However, that average can, and should, encompass a range of one to twenty lines, depending on the issue being discussed.
2 Signposting
   Make the first sentence of each paragraph preview, summarize or lead into that paragraph's main point. The busy reader can then get the sense of the whole passage, by scanning these first sentences. This sounds contrived, but, in fact, it comes easily and naturally.

The passage below is the unparagraphed version of the section in this chapter headed 'How Much Does Presentation Matter?' How would you paragraph it? Check the original to see the effects of the first-sentence signposts.

It is a cliché of modern marketing that an article can and even should cost many times more to package than to produce. Appearance may not be all, but it certainly makes a great difference, and one that can profitably be measured in increased sales. In another context, politicians, too, play the 'image' game, and research into interviewing practices has similarly shown that many interview decisions are heavily influenced by first impressions. The same is true with written material. Professional-looking presentation goes a long way to persuading your reader of your professionalism. Layout which is easy to look at encourages your reader to look and read. How much consideration do *you* give to the appearance of your material? Leaving layout to the typist, or a company 'house style', is to abandon your responsibility and your opportunity.

Figure 3.1 *Paragraphing exercise*

Headings

These, even more than first-sentence signposts, direct the reader's attention to the major issues. They are the reader's road map, showing the overall structure of the document. Good headings are brief (half to three-quarters of a line at most), specific ('Miscellaneous' is not a very helpful heading), and mutually exclusive (the same point should not fall under several headings). Single paragraphs do not normally justify separate headings, but this obviously depends on the content.

Numbering Systems and Lists

Whether or not headings are used, it is often helpful to number sections and sub-sections. Two numbering systems are common:

  1 Numeric:
   1 Section
    1.1 Sub-section
     1.1.1 Point
      1.1.1.1 Sub-point

2 Alphanumeric:
  A Section
    1 Sub-section
      (a) Point
        (i) Sub-point

The first system is the more useful for cross-referencing. With either system, four levels of subdivision should be the maximum, and even that may leave your reader struggling to disentangle your connections.

Items in lists can be numbered according to whichever system you have chosen. Alternatively, you can highlight them with 'blobs' or 'bullet points'. (Open or filled circles or squares, dashes, asterisks, or hash signs, according to your fancy. Not all of them, however!) You can even omit these preliminaries altogether.

Different layouts can give more or less emphasis to lists. You do not *have* to start at the left-hand margin; indenting and even centring the items, particularly short, 'blob-less' ones, can be very effective.

Emphasis

To ensure that the reader who only scans your material does not miss any important points, you may want to emphasize these visually. There are many ways of doing this, although some depend on your typewriter or printer facilities.

– CAPITALS
– <u>underlining</u>
– **Bold or heavier type**

– *italics*
– size
– l e t t e r s p a c i n g
– colour

You may even **COMBINE STYLES.**

But be wary – too much variety dazzles the eye and disengages the brain. Moderation and consistency are to be preferred.

Incidentally, although colour reproduction on to white paper may be too expensive for the majority of us to use regularly, copying onto coloured paper is a cheap and effective way of splitting up and emphasizing different sections of training manuals or even reports.

Numerical Information

I want to consider briefly the presentation of numerical information. The only thing more daunting, for many readers, than a page crammed with closely-written text is one crammed with numbers. Only include those few which are truly essential to your argument.

If possible, display them in chart or tabular form (see Chapter 19 for more details on this); banish them to an appendix rather than incorporating them in the text; and remember KISS.

Short numbers – substitute the word 'million' for a string of noughts, or indicate the order of magnitude of the figures at the beginning of a chart or table.

Simplified numbers – quote 'ballpark' figures, averages and mid-points, and round to three or at most four significant figures (eg not £6,478,329, but £6·48 million, or even £6½ million.) The loss of accuracy is usually more than balanced by the increase in understanding.

Pictures

Another acronym is PUP – Please Use Pictures. These may be charts or tables; they may also be photographs (modern photocopiers reproduce black-and-white photographs quite adequately) or other illustrations. Anything which can save a thousand words has to be welcome, but pictures have other advantages too:

– They attract the reader's eye and, therefore, attention.
– They are often remembered better than words.
– They convey a professional image.

See Chapters 9 and 19 for ideas about illustrations.

CHECKLIST

PRESENTING YOUR MATERIAL

Do you:	OK	Could be better	Should be better
• Consider the appearance of your material?	—	—	—
• Plan the use of white space?	—	—	—
• Have one main topic per paragraph?	—	—	—
• Vary paragraph length?	—	—	—
• Begin each paragraph with 'signpost' sentences?	—	—	—
• Use headings?	—	—	—
• Use a consistent numbering system?	—	—	—
• Display lists effectively?	—	—	—
• Include only essential numbers?	—	—	—
• Present numbers simply?	—	—	—
• Use charts and tables?	—	—	—
• Include detailed information in appendices?	—	—	—
• Use pictures?	—	—	—

4 Editing and Revision

┌───┐

▷   SUMMARY   ◁

- Review and revision are integral parts of the writing task. The most important review is the one from your reader's standpoint, assessing how well your writing will achieve its objective. If possible get other people to perform this review in order to get different reactions.
- The reviewer's ABC stands for Accuracy (of facts, and basic proofreading of grammar, punctuation and spelling), Brevity and Clarity.

└───┘

First Review Level

You have written your final words; the report, case study or job description has been typed; you sigh with relief that your writing task is finished. But it probably is not. Only for short, straightforward documents should the first draft also be the last. The opportunity to review, edit and revise is one great advantage that writing has over speech. However, to be valuable, the review needs to be seen as an integral part of the writing operation, to be planned and tackled systematically.

There are different levels of review. The first and most important is to consider how well the document will achieve your objective. Will your reader be willing and able to:

- Carry out your instructions?
- Agree with your conclusions?

– Support your request for a bigger budget, or whatever your aim is?

Try to dissociate yourself from your own position and put yourself in your reader's place.

– What does your reader need to know in order to achieve your objective? Have you included it?
– In what order will he or she want to consider the points? Have you followed that order?
– Will your reader understand your language? Have you eliminated or explained all jargon?
– What do you expect your reader to do next? Have you said so?

It is better not to carry out this review immediately you have finished writing. Leave it for an hour or two, or even overnight if you can, and you will feel less proprietorial about your work, and more prepared to cut and change as drastically as necessary.

On the other hand, do not be a typist's bane, the writer who continually makes minor alterations which are no great improvement on the original. Such alterations may be much easier with word-processors, but they are still not worth either your or your typist's time.

Getting one or more other people to review the work for you avoids the danger of your merely repeating your previous thought-patterns. It also much increases the likelihood that you will, between you, properly anticipate your reader's response, since a good reviewer will not necessarily agree with you, but will offer you a different perspective. However galling it may be to have your careful arguments rejected, it is better if they are rejected by your reviewer than by your real reader. Be grateful, and seek out that reviewer again.

The Reviewer's Alphabet

The other review levels are A, B and C.

A stands for Accuracy

First, accuracy of facts. Check your sources. Are you making any assumptions, and if so are they valid? Are your numbers right? And any names? What about views or actions attributed to other people? These are all points which are likely to be noticed if incorrect, and to affect your reader's reaction.

Then the basic proofreading for errors of grammar, punctuation and spelling. Most word-processors can check spelling. However, their dictionaries are limited and they only identify spellings not found in the dictionary. This means they will throw up as errors many correct words, and ignore words which exist in the dictionary but are incorrectly spelt in their context eg 'to' instead of 'too'. If in doubt about a word or construction, look it up. And have standard reference works and dictionaries to hand before you begin, or you will be tempted not to bother.

Areas where mistakes are most commonly made are:

– Beginnings	– Small words
– Endings	– Variations from standard copy
– Near other errors	– Additions and corrections.

These are all worth double-checking, as are:

- Names.
- Addresses.
- Numbers.
- Dates.
- Section numbering.
- Lines or paragraphs starting with the same word. (These are often omitted by mistake. Guard against this by reading the text aloud.)
- Consistency of punctuation and layout.

It often helps to proofread with a partner, especially tables or strings of numbers. Frequent breaks improve attentiveness.

B stands for Brevity

Is every point you make worth making? Keep asking yourself 'so what?' and drop the passages which do not add to your argument. Strike out redundant phrases and clichés, making every word earn its place.

Check also for your 'pet' words. We all have them – words like *absolutely, really, actually, however, therefore* or phrases like *by the way, as a result, and so on.* There is nothing wrong with these words and phrases except that we overuse them, often without realizing it. Again this is where it is very useful to have someone else read your writing.

C stands for Clarity

Check the FOG Index of your writing to test how intelligible it is; examine the layout to see how clear and readable it looks; and read the work aloud to make sure it sounds sensible.

CHECKLIST

EDITING AND REVISION

Do you:	OK	Could be better	Should be better
• Review your work?	—	—	—
• Get other people to review it?	—	—	—
• Review from the reader's standpoint?	—	—	—
• Revise as drastically as necessary?	—	—	—
• Avoid constant, minor alterations?	—	—	—
• Check your facts?	—	—	—
• Check your grammar?	—	—	—
• Check your punctuation?	—	—	—
• Check your spelling?	—	—	—
• Double-check error-prone parts?	—	—	—
• Proofread with a partner?	—	—	—
• Ask yourself 'so what?' for each point?	—	—	—
• Eliminate redundancies and pet words?	—	—	—
• Check your FOG Index?	—	—	—
• Check your layout?	—	—	—
• Read your writing aloud?	—	—	—

Part 2 What Trainers Write

5 Job Descriptions, Performance Standards and Performance Objectives

	SUMMARY	

- Job descriptions give a brief yet complete picture of the purpose and functions of a job. To be useful they should be kept 'live' and up-to-date.
- Performance standards identify how well a job should be done. They measure competent performance and focus on the results of the activity. Measures should ideally be quantitative, but that is not always possible. Express qualitative measures as clearly and unambiguously as possible.
- Performance objectives cover one-off tasks and projects. They resemble performance standards in intent and form, except that they must have a target date for achievement of the objective.

Job Descriptions

Job descriptions have a number of purposes:

- To ensure that the job holder and manager understand the job in the same way.
- To provide information about the job to 'outsiders', eg for recruitment or job evaluation.
- To provide an organizational overview which will pinpoint duplication or omission of tasks.

The first purpose is the most important, which suggests that the best people to write job descriptions are the job holder and manager working together. If they write the description themselves, they are much more likely to use it on a day-to-day basis as a 'live' tool, and keep it up-to-date. A large part of the value of the exercise lies also in the discussion necessary to produce the description – it is amazing how often the process of writing a job description brings to light and resolves unacknowledged disagreements about job performance.

Trainers too, acting as job analysts, may write job descriptions, usually after interviewing the job holder and manager concerned. To make sure the jobs are reasonable (managers have been known to propose jobs requiring such vastly different levels of skill that it would be impossible to find them together in one person), consult national competency standards for the job area concerned. These are often based on a framework of typical job functions, for instance, in the training area, identifying training needs. These functions are divided into standard units or activities, arranged in a hierarchy of different job levels. For the training officer job level, identifying training needs might involve gathering information on individual training needs. A training manager might be more concerned with identifying organizational needs.

When it comes to writing the job description, whoever does so, it is important that information is gathered and recorded in a consistent way, and as succinctly as possible. Concentrate throughout on outcomes and results, and how these contribute to the overall purpose of the job. Describe job functions with active (not passive), action verbs. For example:

The job holder runs the following courses, rather than:
The following courses are run, or:
The job holder is concerned with the following courses.

Equally, make your verbs specific. 'Running' a course, in a document addressed to training staff, seems unlikely to be misunderstood; however, you might want to distinguish between actually presenting training sessions and coordinating other people's sessions in a seminar. You might also want to make it clear whether 'running' a course includes, to take some common 'I thought you were doing that' examples:

- Room set-up
- Checking equipment
- Checking visual aids
- Making available enough sets of handout documentation, etc.

As far as is possible *without being too wordy*, job descriptions should dispel any potential ambiguity. Numbers help. It is often useful, if not always easy, to allocate an approximate percentage of time spent on each major activity. These percentages are very unlikely to add up to 100 per cent – anything from 60 per cent to 90 per cent may be realistic depending on the nature and level of the job. To take one example, even a machine operator's job has incalculables such as down time, company or union meetings etc, which could easily account for 10 per cent of time. Managers, at the other extreme, may find as much as 50 per cent of their time difficult to allocate.

There are many formats for job descriptions. One format which is particularly useful for job holders writing their own descriptions is the job analysis questionnaire. It can also be used by job analysts to structure an interview. As with all questionnaires, make the questions clear and specific, allow enough space for the answers, and keep the document as short as possible. Ten-page job analysis questionnaires are daunting for all concerned.

The job analysis questionnaire may well be sufficient as a job description. However, if the descriptions are to be used frequently for recruitment and job evaluation purposes, a more easily comparable format, is helpful. Most organizations have their own preferred approach. One, commendably brief, examples has:

- A front sheet which states the overall purpose of the job, working conditions and required skills.
- A second page (or the reverse of the sheet) for the major responsibilities and functions of the job.

This format has the advantage that the job responsibilities and functions are listed on a single page, which can be pinned up above the work area as a constant reminder. Job descriptions are notorious for being buried in a bottom drawer, and only dusted off for the yearly performance appraisal, if then. The shorter and more visible they are, the better their chance of being kept up-to-date.

Performance Standards

Job descriptions describe *what* the job does; performance standards identify *how well* it should be done.

As with job descriptions, the best people to specify this are the job holder and manager working together. Trainers, however, can help by identifying comparable external standards and by providing models for writing standards.

In the UK, nationwide standards are being specified for all occupations, but organizations may well want to adapt these or to specify their own company-specific performance standards.

The UK Training and Development Standards may usefully serve as a general model. They are in three parts:

1 An 'element of competence', essentially an activity:

   Select, prepare and adapt exercises and simulations to support collaborative learning. Note the action verbs: 'select', 'prepare' and 'adapt'.

   When writing company-specific standards, trainers should match these activities to the job descriptions.

2 'Performance criteria'. These are the core of the standards. They consist of four or five critical outcomes or results for each activity, which, taken together, will tell you if the activity is being performed competently:

   Written support materials (existing, adapted and original) are accurate and in a style and format appropriate to the needs and capabilities of the audience.

3 'Range indicators'. These define the conditions which may qualify the activity, such as available resources, prescribed methods, locations, etc. For example:

   Learning materials: written text, graphical, audio, visual display.

Obviously, national standards are written broadly so as to cover *all* possible aspects of a job. Companies preparing their own standards might wish to modify the format.

In general terms, all performance standards should *measure competent performance*. These three words bear examination.

Measure. Numbers are the best measurements, of course (eg, budget, sales, production statistics, course evaluation ratings), as they are less ambiguous than words. For example:

   Average end-of-course ratings should not be less than:
   – achievement of objectives – 5 out of 6.
   – overall rating – 4 out of 6.

Quantitative measures are not, however, infallible (people can play the numbers game very industriously); nor are they realistically obtainable in all circumstances. How do you measure numerically the success of a relationship? You should also consider whether the criterion is worth measuring – complex control systems monitoring less-than-critical criteria only add to bureaucracy.

Qualitative measures may well be as important as quantitative ones. Unfortunately they are harder to write and, often, to monitor. Write them using specific, concrete language – the fewer the abstractions, the greater the likelihood of common understanding. Examples can be very helpful, provided they are recognized as being just examples, and do not exclude other situations.

For instance, the standard quoted earlier, about written materials being accurate and appropriate to their readers' needs and capabilities, could have as an example:

> **If readers may be unfamiliar with any technical, industry, or company terms or abbreviations, these should be defined on the first occasion they are used in a document.**

Competent. What is competent? Do you set standards to measure the 'best practice', or what is generally OK, or what is only barely acceptable? The answer will vary from one company to another. The important point is that manager and job holder should understand the word in the same way.

Performance. Performance is the outcome of a job, the results, not the input (eg the skill or effort required). That *seems* obvious. Consider as a standard: **Written support materials should be prepared with care and effort.** This standard could be met by materials which were completely unsuitable for their purpose, and some very effective materials may be produced with comparatively little effort. And how do you measure care and effort anyway? But input criteria may become important (and contentious) when standards are used in performance appraisal. It is human nature to want hard work recognized and rewarded (even if it was unproductive!). In some situations, input criteria can be useful; just don't let them creep in without being aware of what you are doing.

One final point to consider with performance standards, is that some outcomes are more important than others. If you want to get sophisticated, you can weight your standards – in particular if they are used to determine financial reward.

Performance Objectives

Many companies have formal performance measurement systems which embrace both standards and objectives. Whether or not you work to a formal system, both standards and objectives are useful tools for trainers and managers.

51

Performance standards cover the regular job activities. Objectives refer to one-off tasks, projects and goals, either job-related (**Prepare a course to meet managers' needs for negotiation skills**), or for personal development (**Improve your negotiation skills**). All the comments made above about measuring competent performance apply equally to performance objectives. The main difference in writing standards and objectives is that objectives need a target date.

> **Prepare a course to meet managers' needs for negotiation skills by 31 March 1992.**
> **Improve your negotiation skills by 30 June 1992.**

6 Procedures, Job Aids and Manuals

▷   SUMMARY   ◁

- A company-wide and controlled method of writing procedures will avoid duplication, omission and confusion. Essential elements are standardized procedure layout, standardized reference coding, review and control. Also important are clear objectives, systematic design, and language which is consistent and appropriate to the user.
- Job aids may be considered as mini-procedures. They give brief but detailed information on how to perform a particular function.
- Lengthy procedures, or collections of related procedures may become training and reference manuals. These need to be laid out and indexed for easy use.

Procedures

I will practise what I am about to preach, by setting out guidelines for writing procedures in the form of a procedure.

Ref no: A-326-001   *Title:* WRITING PROCEDURES
Written by: N. Stimson   *Date written:* 1/91
Approved by: P. Edwards   *Date revised:* 4/91

Distribution: All managers and supervisors

	See also	*Rev*

1.0 OBJECTIVE
To provide a guide to writing procedures, covering format, design, style and control.

2.0 FORMAT

2.1 CONSISTENCY
Unlike job aids, procedures should not be produced in different sizes and formats. Their primary purposes are training and reference, rather than acting as on-the-job reminders; a consistent format allows users to track down information easily.   *below*

2.2 LEFT-HAND FACING PAGES
Procedures should normally be held in binders so that they can be opened flat with both left- and right-hand facing pages visible. Print the procedures only on right-hand pages, and reserve the left-hand ones for reproducing any relevant charts, diagrams, forms etc, which are referred to on that page of the procedures. Photo-reducing these will enable you to add pointers and comments.

2.3 COLUMNS
Use the column on the left for section and subsection numbering, and those on the right for cross-references and highlighting revisions.

2.4 REFERENCE NUMBERING
Some sort of standard company-wide reference numbering system is necessary for most companies, but keep it as simple as possible and use existing codes which people already know. The reference for this document, A-326-001, stands for:

Ref no: A-326-001   *Title:* WRITING PROCEDURES

	See also	*Rev*

A – Administration, a major class of procedures. Other typical categories might be Finance, Production, Maintenance, etc. These could be denoted either by a letter or number code.

326 – departmental cost code for Training Department.

001 – procedure number, unique within Training Department procedures.

3.0 DESIGN

3.1 OBJECTIVES SECTION

This should tell the reader what the procedure covers, and what any user of the procedure should be able to do.

as in 1.0 above

3.2 DESIGN STEPS

3.2.1 For each operation in the procedure, ask yourself:

What is being done now?

WHAT ELSE MIGHT BE DONE INSTEAD?

Who does it?

WHO ELSE MIGHT DO IT INSTEAD?

Where is it done?

WHERE ELSE INSTEAD?

When is it done?

WHEN ELSE INSTEAD?

How is it done?

HOW ELSE INSTEAD?

3.2.2 For each operation, identify what information, equipment, materials are necessary for the operation to be performed.

3.2.3 For each operation, identify and, where appropriate, design the output format.

Ref no: A-326-001   *Title:* WRITING PROCEDURES

	See also	*Rev*

3.2.4 Identify clearly, by job title, who performs and who may authorize each operation.

3.2.5 Sequence the operations, highlighting any parallel or alternative operations. Flowcharts are easy to follow and understand.   **Ch 19**

3.2.6 Consider the treatment of exceptions. You may want to put these in an appendix rather than in the main procedure.

3.2.7 Consider whether to repeat information which is held elsewhere or just cross-reference it. Remember that all procedures should be able to stand alone and enable the user to perform the operation.

3.3 KEY DESIGN CRITERIA

Identify clearly any important factors and their impact on the operations. These might include:

– Legal requirements.
– Safety precautions.
– Security.
– Confidentiality.
– Quality control.
– Audit controls.
– Management information requirements.
– Job flexibility requirements.

4.0 STYLE

4.1 SECTIONS AND PARAGRAPHS

4.1.1 As far as possible, give each section or subsection a separate, unique heading. Use consistent text enhancements (capitals, underlining, bold print) to identify them.   **Ch 3**

Ref no: A-326-001   *Title:* WRITING PROCEDURES

	See also	*Rev*

4.1.2 Use a numeric section numbering system, as in this procedure.	Ch 3	
4.1.3 Each process or action should constitute a separate line or paragraph.		
4.2 CHOICE OF WORDS	Ch 2	
4.2.1 Use the imperative or present tense, second person ('you').		
4.2.2 Keep terminology consistent (eg do not refer to both 'billing' and 'invoicing' for the same process). Frequent repetition of the same term is stylistically acceptable.		
4.2.3 Refer to forms, procedures and reports by title and any reference number.		
4.2.4 Choose language appropriate to the user – technical jargon **is** appropriate if the user will understand it.		
5.0 CONTROL		
5.1 REVIEW AND APPROVAL		
All procedures should be reviewed by the user and approved by the immediate supervisor. Procedures which span several areas of operation should be approved at the appropriate level of authority.		4/91
5.2 UPDATING		
5.2.1 Users should notify the procedure writer of any on-going revisions which are needed.		
5.2.2 The procedure writer should *immediately* revise the procedure to incorporate any major changes, eg new equipment, new format of input or output, new or significant changes in activities.		4/91

Ref no: A-326-001   *Title:* WRITING PROCEDURES

	See also	*Rev*

5.2.3 The procedure writer should review the procedure regularly in order to include any less urgent changes, eg new job titles, minor changes in activities.

5.2.4 Revised pages should be re-issued to all procedure-holders with a covering note indicating the changes; for extensive amendments reissue the whole procedure.

5.3   CENTRAL MONITORING

If the master copies of all procedures are held centrally, they can be monitored to:

- Identify any duplication of activities.
- Highlight areas where procedures do not exist.
- Ensure proper approval and authorization.
- Ensure that they are kept up-to-date.
- Check consistency of writing.

Job Aids

Trainers may also need to write job aids for employees, either to reinforce training in a task or procedure, or following a general analysis of the job. Job aids are more detailed than job descriptions or even procedures, but normally only cover a single task. Their function is to remind the employee of what needs to be done. They therefore have to be written with the employee constantly in mind, and must take account of his or her previous knowledge, or lack of it. They are particularly useful for critical or infrequent tasks, and are often written as checklists, flowcharts, decision trees or step-by-step instructions. Whatever format is chosen, the following structure is useful to ensure no major points are missed:

1 Preparation
What needs to be known or done before the task can be performed; what information, materials or equipment need to be ready. Diagrams may sometimes be helpful.

2 Start-up
Any preliminaries to the task, including commissioning or setting equipment into operation.

3 Task
All steps, in order of performance. You normally need to do the task yourself, maybe several times, before writing the instructions. Include only essential details, but enough to enable the task to be completed.

4 Close-down
Finishing procedures, including any decommissioning of equipment, recording of results or reporting to other people.

Language *must* be clearly understood. Avoid elegant sentences: short phrases, each covering a single point, will be followed more easily. If employees' reading ability is limited, use step-by-step diagrams, but express the instructions briefly in words too. And just to make sure the job aid is as foolproof as you think, test it out on typical employees beforehand.

Since job aids exist to help the employee actually perform the task, they should not be filed away in a manual. They are more useful pinned on the wall above the piece of equipment to be operated, or stuck at the front of a record or log book.

Presentation is therefore paramount. Job aids which are attached to equipment should be bright, easy-to-read posters, laminated for cleanliness and durability. Even job aids for clerical procedures benefit from being covered in transparent protective material, if they are likely to be used frequently. And size may also be important. A5 or credit-card-sized reminders, which fit employees' personal filing systems, are more likely to be carried and referred to regularly.

The job aid shown in Figure 6.1 could be used by training officers (or anyone else setting up a course). It could be displayed in the training room or where the course materials are stored.

TRAINING COURSE SET-UP

If possible set up the training room the night before a course. Consider:

- Arrangement of furniture.
- Placing of equipment:
  - CAN EVERYONE SEE EVERYTHING?
- Safety and security:
  - UNPLUG / SWITCH OFF ALL ELECTRICAL CONNECTIONS AT NIGHT.
  - CHECK NO TRAILING LEADS.
  - LOCK TRAINING ROOM OVERNIGHT.
- Equipment back-up:
  - Spare bulbs   - Fuses
- Materials for each participant:
  - Nameplates   - Handouts
  - Pads   - Manuals
  - Pencils
- Standard materials:
  - Flip chart pads   - Adhesive tape
  - Flip chart pens   - Paper clips
  - Gum for posting flip - Stapler
    chart sheets on walls - Hole punch
- Visuals and course notes for trainer.
- Refreshments.

Figure 6.1 *Job aid*

Manuals

Procedure manuals usually consist of collections of related procedures. It is helpful to include reference aids such as contents pages and indexes.

Contents pages are easy to include and keep up to date. If the procedures are well-established and unlikely to change frequently, it is useful to have sequential page numbering through all the documents; otherwise the page reference has to include the procedure number too.

Ref no	*Procedure*	*Page*
A-326-010	Introduction	1
A-326-011	Identifying training needs	3
A-326-012	Preparing the training agenda	7
A-326-013	Recording and confirming course nominations	11

Figure 6.2 *Contents page of a Training Department Procedures manual*

In this example, the second page of 'Preparing the training agenda' would be page 8. However, if each procedure was numbered separately, it would be page A-326-012/2.

Indexes are considerably more complicated. They can be created manually, by scanning each page and picking out the main points. This is tedious and time-consuming. Fortunately, they can also be created by using word processors to find key words.

Updating indexes is also a major job. You not only have to include references to the changed elements of the procedures, but inserted passages may also have caused page numbering changes. This is where separate page numbering for each procedure is valuable, otherwise you may need to renumber all the pages of subsequent procedures. In any case, it is often necessary to re-create the index completely each time there are changes, so it is sensible to restrict indexes, where possible, to the well-established procedures.

7 Forms and Questionnaires

▷   SUMMARY   ◁

Forms and questionnaires are often difficult to design as they have multiple users – the people who fill in the information and those who interpret it.

KISS is the key word; attractive layout is also extremely important.

This chapter considers:

- Forms
- Simple questionnaires
- Attitude surveys
- Tests

Forms

Trainers may need to design forms for various purposes, both for their own use and for that of one or more other people. It is therefore critical to identify the *most important* reader or user of the form. For instance, with a job application form, is it the applicant or the recruiter? Surely the applicant, but most application forms are designed for organizational convenience.

Taking a performance appraisal form as another example, is the most important user:

- The manager who completes the report?
- The employee who receives a copy?
- The 'grandfather' manager or other organizational watchdog?
- The training officer who extracts training needs?
- The personnel officer who translates performance ratings into salary figures?

Depending on the scheme, it could be any of them, although most schemes would *say* it was the employee. This is often not reflected in the forms, which may be heavy on demographic information (division, department, region, grade, length of service, age, job history, etc), and consist of a formidable array of performance rating boxes with little or no room for comments.

So, establishing the prime user and their needs is the necessary starting point. Keeping It as Short and Simple as possible is a need *all* users share, but one which is often sacrificed in the inevitably doomed attempt to satisfy everyone. Ruthless pruning is normally the best policy, if necessary creating two simple forms for different users rather than one complex one.

Let us consider a few important elements of forms design and see how they are illustrated in a performance appraisal form (Figure 7.1).

Boxes should be large enough for manual or typewritten completion and there should be enough space for comments. Typewriters or word-processors may not allow enough flexibility of layout for forms design – if the form will be in frequent use, it is worth having it printed or using a specialized computer package.

If completion instructions are necessary, they should be on the form itself. A smaller typeface is usually acceptable for these, provided that it can still be read when photocopied or faxed!

If the form includes ratings, beware of the common 'central tendency' – picking the middle-of-the-road option every time. Having an even number of ratings (four or six, rather than five) reduces this. Incidentally, no matter how many rating options you offer, some people will nevertheless put their mark between the boxes, so you do need to consider how you will interpret that.

EXPLANATION OF RATINGS

Not meeting basic job requirements: This does not necessarily imply poor employee performance – it may result from other factors e.g. postponing certain major activities because of changing priorities.

Meeting job requirements: This indicates consistently satisfactory performance of all major job areas.

Exceeding job requirements: This should be used when the whole job is being consistently performed at a fully satisfactory level, and some important areas at a significantly higher level.

Outstanding: This indicates exceptional performance.

Ratings should be amplified with comments as appropriate.

OVERALL RATING OF PERFORMANCE

Not meeting basic job requirements	Meeting job requirements	Exceeding job requirements	Outstanding

COMMENTS

Figure 7.1 *Performance appraisal rating form*

EVALUATION QUESTIONNAIRE FOR SESSION CONTENT AND INSTRUCTOR

Weigh the two statements and decide where along the scale of 6-5-4-3-2-1 the most accurate description lies. Here is what each number stands for:

'6' STRONGLY AGREE with the statement at the LEFT
'5' SOMEWHAT AGREE with the statement at the LEFT
'4' or '3' Neither statement alone is accurate - answer lies in the middle
'2' SOMEWHAT AGREE with the statement at the RIGHT
'1' STRONGLY AGREE with the statement at the RIGHT

CIRCLE THE number that best described your thought. If a statement does not apply, leave it blank.

EXAMPLE:

c)	I learned something new	6-5-4-3-2-1	c)	I learned nothing new
k)	The room was ideal for this session	6-5-4-3-2-1	k)	The room was inadequate

a)	Subject of the session directly related to my needs	6-5-4-3-2-1	a)	I have no need for the subject offered
b)	The objective of the session was met	6-5-4-3-2-1	b)	The objective was not met
c)	I learned something new	6-5-4-3-2-1	c)	I learned nothing new
d)	The session covers the right amount of material	6-5-4-3-2-1	d)	The session covers too much/too little material*
e)	Session material is well organised	6-5-4-3-2-1	e)	Topics seem out of order
f)	Explanations were clear and simple	6-5-4-3-2-1	f)	Unclear, confusing explanations
g)	The session was alive and interesting	6-5-4-3-2-1	g)	The session was dull
h)	Reading material was outstanding	6-5-4-3-2-1	h)	Reading material was poor
i)	Exercises were helpful and stimulating	6-5-4-3-2-1	i)	Exercises were not helpful
j)	Visual aids were outstanding	6-5-4-3-2-1	j)	Visual aids were poor/not used*
k)	The room was ideal for this session	6-5-4-3-2-1	k)	The room was inadequate
l)	Overall the session was outstanding	6-5-4-3-2-1	l)	Session was worthless

* Delete as appropriate

Figure 7.2 *End-of-course rating sheet*

Questionnaires

These are used and often designed by trainers for various purposes. Common examples are a simple training-needs survey, a job analysis questionnaire or an end-of-course rating sheet. Such questionnaires as these are fairly straightforward to design, even where they contain rating scales.

More specialized questionnaires may be needed for attitude surveys or to identify skills and abilities. While these are not necessarily difficult to devise, interpretation is often critical and the design of the questionnaire can affect the results. Major surveys or ability tests should be left to specialists, but you may want to prepare smaller-scale ones yourself.

Attitude Surveys

EMPLOYEE OPINION QUESTIONNAIRE

Please read each item below. Tick the extent to which you agree or disagree with the statement made and circle the importance rating you give to the item. Your response should reflect your view of X overall, not just your own situation.

	Agree		*Disagree*		*Importance*
	Fully	Partly	Partly	Fully	(Scale 1-low 3-high)
1. Morale is high.	[]	[]	[]	[]	1 2 3
2. Managers use their time well.	[]	[]	[]	[]	1 2 3
3. When mistakes are made, we try to learn from them.	[]	[]	[]	[]	1 2 3
4. Staff are usually involved in decisions which directly affect their work.	[]	[]	[]	[]	1 2 3
5. In X quality is of the highest importance.	[]	[]	[]	[]	1 2 3

Figure 7.3 *Start of attitude survey*

Points to bear in mind when designing an attitude survey are:

- Since completion is often voluntary, the survey *must be attractive and easy to complete*. Unclear instructions, too many questions, fuzzy printing, asking for demographic information which will identify individual respondents – all these are likely to reduce your completion rate significantly. Spelling out the purpose of the survey, and how and when you will tell respondents of the results, will make people take it seriously.
- *You* are likely to be the person collating and interpreting the results, so make it as easy as possible. If the analysis is to be done manually, avoid as much calculation as you can. If you will be using a computer package, such as a simple spreadsheet package, consider in advance how you will lay out the information, how it needs to be sorted, and what combination of factors you will use for analysis. You may want to seek the help of the computer department.

The attitude survey in Figure 7.3 was in large part analysed manually. Points were allotted to each response (fully agree +2, partly agree +1, partly disagree −1, fully disagree −2), and these multiplied by the importance rating (1, 2 or 3). A number of questions covered the same main topics, eg motivation, efficiency, quality-consciousness. The replies were analysed both on an individual question basis and according to topic. With about 200 replies, this was tedious but possible. With more, it would have been impossible. Even so, only limited demographic analyses could be managed, eg by region or category of staff.

- Where you can, express questions positively. This is easier to understand than a tangle of double negatives.
- You will get a more accurate picture if 'right' answers do not always have the same rating; otherwise respondents will get into the habit of answering, say, 5 or 6, and will not think about each question. It is better for the 'right' answer to be 6 for one question and 1 for the next. However, this does make manual collation of results considerably more difficult – that is why the example end-of-course rating sheet and employee opinion questionnaire both disregard this principle.
- If possible, use a weighting factor so that respondents can identify how important they consider a factor as well as how they rate it. Again, this makes manual collation of results more difficult.

In the case of this employee opinion questionnaire, however,

it was well worth doing, as the importance ratings changed the overall picture significantly.
- Decide in advance how you will deal with incorrectly- completed questionnaires. It is common for people to give ratings between boxes, or even beyond the end of a scale.
- Test the questionnaire for ease of completion and interpretation before printing and issuing it. If it is confidential, test it on someone outside your company.
- Be cautious in interpreting the results, especially of a one-off survey. People may be wary of what is expected of them, and say what they think you want to hear rather than what they really think. Repeat surveys, highlighting any changes in attitude, are usually more valid.
- *Do* publish the results, whatever they are. Secrecy destroys trust.

Tests

The aim with most test questionnaires is not to pass or fail the people taking the test, but to provide information about them and their level of knowledge or aptitude in certain areas.

Tests of knowledge are comparatively straightforward to prepare. Different types of questions will establish different degrees of knowledge. Multiple choice, matching or true/false questions are good for discrimination and simple relationships. For example:

Which is the correct spelling?
questionaire questionere questionnaire

Essay questions will identify depth of understanding, but are slower and more difficult to assess:

To what extent ...
Compare and contrast ...
Examine the effects of ...

Knowledge tests are better if they are short and selective, than if they try to be comprehensive. Make sure that the questions are clear (test all tests before using them), and that they cover the most important and most commonly needed areas – not the most abstruse ones. Formulation of questions is covered in more detail in Chapter 11.

Psychological tests are not for amateurs to design or use, and some 'communication skills' or 'leadership style' questionnaires are similar in sensitivity. Many such instruments are available commercially. Their validity varies and interpretation of results should be handled with caution.

You may be tempted to customize them for your own organization, but don't. It is a breach of copyright (unless permission is received) and destroys whatever validity the test has. If you need a serious test specific to your own organization, get it designed by experts, but remember that, for any reliable interpretation of results, it would need to be validated with a sample population. This can take a long time.

There is no reason, however, why you should not design your own light-hearted quizzes. While these would not pretend to be a scientific measure, they can still give valuable insights into behaviour or skills. Make them fun and quick to complete, and do not forget that they are at best only indicators.

	Always	Often	Fairly often	Less often	Rarely	Never

How often do you:
- Identify your reader's needs and attitudes before you start writing?
- Write down your objective before you start writing?
- Write down some sort of plan or structure before you start writing?
- Consciously choose simple words?
- Check your FOG Index?
- Plan the visual presentation of your writing?
- Get someone else to review your writing?

Score: 5 for each **Always**; 4 for each **Often**; 3 for each **Fairly often**; 2 for each **Less often**; 1 for each **Rarely**; 0 for each **Never**.

If you scored:

31 – 35	Wonderful! (Who am I to cast doubts on your veracity?)
21 – 30	Very good. I hope your writing generally meets with the approval and success it deserves.
11 – 20	I expect most people will fall into this category. Why not use this quiz as a writing checklist and push up your score?
5 – 10	It really is worth trying out these tips. You will find your writing much more likely to achieve what you want.
0 – 4	Oh dear! I *am* glad you bought this book.

Figure 7.4 *Writing skills quiz*

8 Course Notes

> SUMMARY <

This chapter covers: joining instructions, the trainer's own notes for running a course, and the trainer's review of the course.
- Joining instructions should be short, welcoming in tone, and include all administrative details and any pre-course work or checklists.
- Trainer's notes, often called a Lesson or Teaching Plan, may be written on paper or cue-cards. A standard 4-column approach (time, content, exercises, A-V aids) is useful.
- The trainer's review of the course should be written for ease of reference and follow-up.

Joining Instructions

Joining instructions are often a trainer's first contact with course participants – they strongly influence the expectations for the course and therefore its ultimate success.

They are a short (1 page maximum?) memo or letter sent before the event to all participants, advising them where and when the course will be held. The formality of the word 'instructions' rather belies their purpose, which is to welcome participants and reinforce their desire to benefit from the course. Depending on the participants and the course itself, this may be done by allaying anxieties, detailing individual and company benefits, or pointing out an urgent need.

Welcome to the 'Presentation Skills for Managers' course, which will be held on 11 and 12 July 1991 in the Gloucester Room, Royal Hotel. Venue details and a timetable are attached.

In a recent survey, making presentations was rated third out of fifteen skills 'most likely to improve managers' career prospects' – well above technical and many management skills. It was also rated top of the 'managers' most hated activities' list! The aim of these two days is to boost your career prospects while persuading you that presentations can be fun. Some common concerns are:

I am not a 'born presenter.' Very few people are, and even they have developed their skills with practice. *Anyone* can be taught to give a workmanlike, professional presentation. Remember, a presenter is not an actor and a presentation is not a performance.

I am too nervous to stand up and speak in front of others. Good preparation breeds confidence, as you will realize for yourself. (Incidentally, it is a myth that nerves are a liability; well managed, nervousness can be a big asset!)

I don't have the time to spend weeks preparing a presentation. You don't need to. *Good* preparation is essential, but a planned approach leading to a successful presentation will actually save you time.

You may have other concerns or there may be particular points on which you want to focus. This is *your* course, and the timetable is flexible enough to allow us to concentrate on people's individual needs. During the course you will prepare and deliver two presentations to the rest of the group, one of 5 minutes and one of 15 minutes. You will decide your topic for your short presentation in the course, but you will find it useful to have a topic in mind beforehand for the longer one. (Keep it simple – you will be amazed at how little you can cover!) If possible, choose a presentation you will use in the future, and *bring with you to the course any reference material you may need.*

The attached checklist can help you identify your personal needs – it is primarily for your own use, although you may wish to share it with your manager. A brief discussion with your manager before the course, to establish what *you* want to get out of these two days, will ensure that you get the most benefit.

I look forward to seeing you on Thursday 11 July 1991 at 9.00 am. Please give me a ring if you have any questions.

Figure 8.1 *Joining memo for internally run Presentation Skills course*

Other purposes of the joining instructions include helping participants gain the most benefit from the course, by suggesting pre-course assignments, checklists, and briefing sessions with participants' managers or course tutors. Also, obviously, timetables and administrative arrangements should be made clear, including a map if the venue is difficult to find. These aspects may be covered in separate attachments to the memo or letter.

Trainer's Notes

The purpose of these is to enable the trainer to run the course.

This is not a book on how to prepare a course, so it would not be appropriate to go into detail about training objectives, course structure, different training techniques etc. As a quick reminder, however:

- Write behavioural training objectives *first*.
  The UK *National Standards for Training and Development* stress that 'learning objectives [should be] derived from an appropriate and relevant analysis of the requirements of the role'.
  For the Presentation Skills course you might have:

  Participants will (a useful introduction as it forces you to identify the behaviour change, and express it as a verb):

  - **identify the needs of their audience.**
  - **identify the objective of their presentation to meet those needs.**
  - **identify how to test that the objective has been met**
  - **plan and structure their presentation to meet their objective.**

- Then work out how to test that these have been achieved, and write the test (even if you do not plan to administer it in that form).
  Eg, writing objectives, analysing a lesson plan, giving presentations.
- Next identify what information participants **must** know to complete the test (and, if you wish, 'should know' and 'nice to know' elements).
  Eg, how to write a behavioural objective, verbs to use and avoid in writing objectives, etc.
- Start by arousing interest. (Explaining the course objectives and describing what you will cover may be less entertaining than a

brilliant multi-media demonstration or witty jokes, but the straightforward approach often works just as well.)
- Break the ice quickly, by getting participants talking and doing things.
  Eg, the paired introductions exercise in the lesson plan below.
- Structure 'must know' items (and any others you decide to include) from the *student's* perspective.
- Summarize frequently.
- Make obvious the links between different topics. Eg, using the introductions exercise as a presentation model, as in the lesson plan below.
- Select the techniques and audio-visual aids which will best reinforce each training point. (See Chapter 9.)
- End on a high note and emphasize the links back to the work situation.
  Eg, make the final exercise a 'real life' one, a presentation they will really have to give.

Many trainers have their own preferred way of setting out these notes but, whatever the format, the following information should be included:

- The basic content which is being covered and the methods used (eg lecture, question-and-answer, etc).
- Links between the content and any audio-visual aids, handouts and exercises.
- Time checks along the way.

Initially this information may be written in some detail as a lesson or teaching plan, which can be preserved for other trainers.
  Points to consider include:

- Objective, equipment and materials information is found on the first sheet only, not on continuation sheets.
- Timings can be estimated either as actual times, as in the example, or elapsed time from the beginning of the session (or both, use colour to distinguish between them).
- The content column can be as explicit or as cryptic as you wish. (However it should not be so cryptic that other trainers cannot use the notes. Emergencies do happen.) Highlighting, in different colours, lecture portions, questions, desired answers, and activities gives a useful overview of the anticipated dynamics of the course, and indicates where any time savings can be made.

LESSON PLAN   Page 1 of 30

Title: Presentation Skills for Managers   Date: 6/91

Objective: Participants will develop their presentation skills and employ good preparation and presentation techniques.

Equipment: Overhead projector, slide projector, flip chart, video recorder (VHS) and TV.

Materials: 25 overhead transparencies (Tr 1 – 25), 32 slides (Sl 1 – 32), 12 handouts (A – L), video.

Time	Content	Exercises	A-V aids
9.00	Welcome. Introduce self. Course arrangements		Trans 1
9.05	Participants to exchange information in pairs and introduce neighbour.	Pair ex	
9.25	Use 'introductions' exercise as presentation model. 4 focuses: – audience – objective – information – presentation		Flip ch
9.30	Presentation only tip of iceberg		Trans 2

Figure 8.2 *Trainer's lesson plan for start of Presentation Skills course*

- Handouts are often associated with exercises, so may be referred to in that column. It is useful to give them an identifying letter or number.
- Similarly, number overhead transparencies and slides to avoid confusion.

If you wish, the material can be abbreviated on to:

- Cue cards.
- Overhead transparency frames.
- A single piece of cardboard (eg the back of an A4 pad). This serves as a complete 1-day-at-a-glance route map of the course, and is also useful for systematically concealing/revealing information on overhead transparencies. (NB Cardboard is better

75

than paper for this purpose, as it is not blown off by the overhead projector fan. However the trainer cannot see the concealed material through it.)

Here is the same lesson plan material abbreviated for cue cards.

PRESENTATION SKILLS
FOR MANAGERS (1)

TIME		EX	A-V
9.00	WELCOME		1
	PAIRED INTRODUCTIONS	PAIRS	
9.25	USE INTROS AS MODEL 4 FOCUSES		F/C
	ICEBERG		2

Figure 8.3 *Trainer's cue card for start of Presentation Skills course*

Trainer's Review of the Course

Most trainers evaluate for themselves the success or otherwise of a course or other learning event. Systematically recording these evaluations has a number of benefits:

- Preparing statistical analyses of training becomes a much simpler task.
- Necessary actions or changes to the course or learning event are less likely to be left to the last minute, or even forgotten.
- Other trainers can appreciate how the course or learning event has developed, and anticipate the likely expectations and reactions of participants.

Figure 8.4 suggests a number of headings which may be helpful in structuring the information. A 'who and when' action column is particularly useful for following-up and ensuring that the actions really happen.

PRESENTATION SKILLS FOR MANAGERS

Date held: 11 – 12 July 1991
Venue: Gloucester Room, Royal Hotel
Tutor: Martin Johnson
Participants: B. Baker (Accounts)
    R. Black (Marketing)
    J. Brown   "
    A. Green   "
    P. Robinson (Accounts)
    H. Smith (Data Processing)
Drop-outs: C. James (Accounts – sickness)
Costs: Direct – £400
    Indirect – 3 trainer days, 1/2 clerical support day, 2 participant days per participant

Comments	Action	
	Who	**When**
Administration – OK		
Venue – Room too small and noisy, hotel services efficient – get different room next time	AS	Next course
Course content – generally OK. Initial planning exercises too easy for this group – develop graded exercises?	MJ	Before next course
Participant reactions – generally OK. Strong initial resistance Black and Green. (NB Did their manager imply course was criticism? – find excuse to talk with manager)	MJ	
Average participant ratings –		
Achievement course objective: 5/6		
Learnt something new: 6/6		
Overall benefit: 5/6		
Follow-up – survey participants and their managers	MJ	Sept 91

Figure 8.4 *Trainer's review of course*

9 **Course Visuals**

▷   SUMMARY   ◁

- When producing visuals, KISS (Keep It Short and Simple) and PUP (Please Use Pictures) are more than guidelines – they become rules. A third rule is to use colour, both to enliven the visual and to emphasize particular points.
- Overhead transparencies are very commonly used visuals; they are a very flexible medium, comparatively easy to prepare, and provide ready-made session handouts. Special materials and the use of computer graphics increase the professional effect, while overlay techniques hold the audience's attention as the message builds up.
- The principles for preparing 35mm slides are similar to those for overhead transparencies. The medium, though less flexible than the overhead projector, can give a more dramatic and professional impression – qualities which should be exploited both in the visual presentation and the accompanying narrative.
- Other common visual aids include flip charts and posters.

Rule 1 – KISS

K eep
I t
S hort and
S imple

HORIZONTAL VISUALS

Six or fewer words per line
Six or fewer words per line

Four or fewer lines per visual
Four or fewer lines per visual

VERTICAL VISUALS

Three words – maximum
Three words – maximum
Three words – maximum
Three words – maximum

Eight lines – maximum
Eight lines – maximum
Eight lines – maximum
Eight lines – maximum

Figure 9.1 *How short is short?*

This is an ideal. Nobody keeps to it all the time, but it is amazing how much information can be condensed into twenty-four (or fewer) words.

WHY WRITE?

- PERMANENT RECORD
- FORMALITY
- CONVEYS "SAME" MESSAGE TO MANY PEOPLE
- CHEAP (?)
- CONTROL OF TIMING

• TO BE READ

Figure 9.2 *Eighteen word visual*

Incidentally, a comment on lettering. This visual is presented in capital letters. Some people like this, as it makes the visual look more regular and uniform. Others maintain that a mixture of upper- and lower-case letters (as in normal print) is easier to read and understand, especially if complete sentences, eg a definition, is being shown. Which do you prefer?

Why Write?

- permanent record
- formality
- conveys "same" message to many people
- cheap (?)
- control of timing
- **to be read**

Figure 9.3 *Visual with lower-case lettering*

Other thoughts raised by these visuals are:

- The use of blobs or bullet points. These attract your audience's attention and make the points easier to absorb and remember. If the order of the points is important, number them instead.
- Enclosing your words in a box, which also focuses the audience's attention.

Rule 2 – PUP

P lease
U se
P ictures

You can, of course, avoid the upper- and lower case dilemma completely by using pictures rather than words. There are many sources of ready-made pictures:

- Posters and photographs.
- Computer graphics packages, which often have a gallery of standard drawings, including people, maps, forms of transport, common objects and symbols. These are a tremendous help in producing sophisticated effects simply.
- Volumes of line drawings and cartoons on which copyright has been waived. These are readily available and an excellent source of ideas, as well as of the pictures themselves.

And you can even draw the pictures yourself. You do not need to be a Rembrandt. Stick men cartoons can be very effective.

Figure 9.4 *Cartoon graphics illustrating successful and unsuccessful communication*

These graphics could be computer produced, or drawn by hand however limited your artistic talent! As an overhead transparency, this could be built up by overlaying the three responses in turn.

Rule 3 – Colour

Colour strengthens visuals enormously, and it can also be used to emphasize or even make points for you, without your needing to spell them out. For instance, if you are gathering ideas at the flipchart, different colours will enable you to classify them as you go, into, say, advantages and disadvantages.

However do avoid the pitfall of colour-blindness. 1 in 12 males cannot distinguish clearly between red and green.

Overhead Transparencies

The favourite medium of many trainers, overhead transparencies are convenient, quick and easy to prepare. Therein lie both their advantages and their – very considerable – disadvantages. It is all too tempting to pile masses of information (instructions and procedures, forms, tables of numbers etc) on to a single transparency, and use it almost as a lesson plan to take you through a fifteen-minute lecturette – tempting but disastrous.

It is so easy to produce a transparency from any document, simply by photocopying, that you can forget that the audience's needs are different. Written documents are primarily meant for individual study at the reader's own pace; overhead transparencies illustrate and emphasize points made at the trainer's or the group's pace.

To control this pace, only key words or small amounts of information should be shown at any time. Procedures, forms, charts and tables of numbers, all need to be broken down into smaller units which are presented separately. I must admit that I do not always stick to the 24-word maximum I have suggested above, but I do try to use it as a guide.

Small units can sometimes be built up using overlay techniques to give the complete information. Otherwise, if you have to present an overall visual impression of the whole document, do so at the end or just hand it out.

Do not, however, go to the other extreme and have a few words or a small picture lost in acres of empty space in the middle of your transparency – unless, of course, you are trying to achieve a particular effect. As a general rule, try to fill the screen.

Always use large, bold lettering for overhead transparencies. There are several lettering systems ranging from computer-produced fonts to manual techniques such as dry transfer or stencils. Even free-hand lettering can look neat and professional if squared paper is used underneath as a guide.

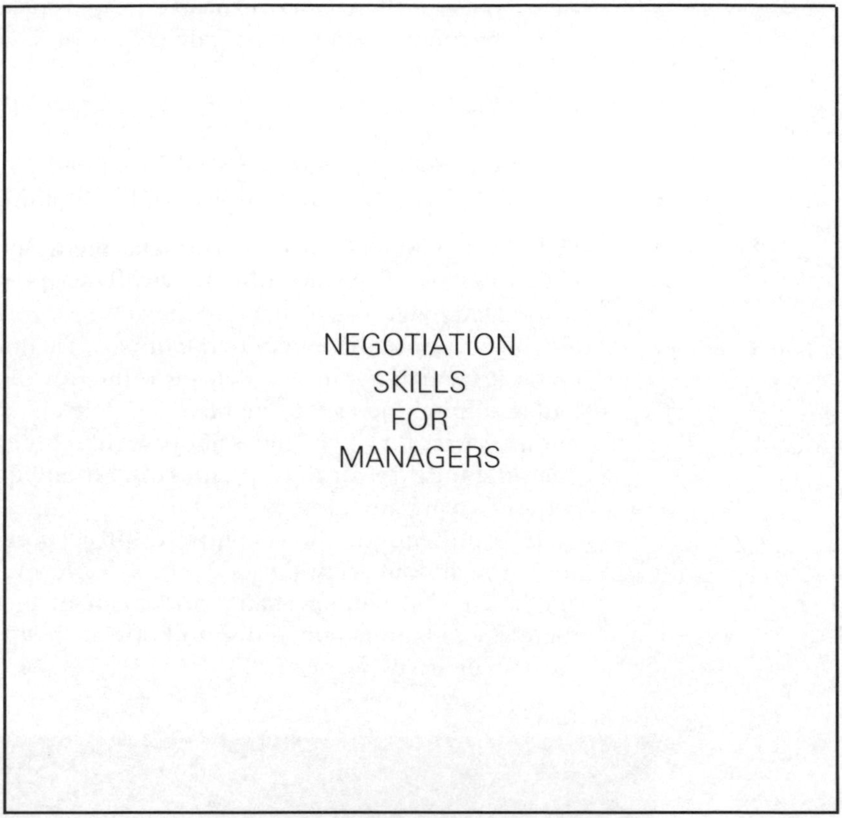

NEGOTIATION
SKILLS
FOR
MANAGERS

Figure 9.5 *Bad overhead transparency*

Colour adds to the impact. Computer graphics can now often be used to produce overhead transparencies in a variety of colours, but even if you do not have these facilities, many of the available materials offer different background colours, different colours on a clear background, and reverse-image effects. And there are also, of course, coloured pens for highlighting or free-hand work.

Overhead transparencies make convenient handouts, too, simply by photocopying the original used to produce the transparency.

Slides

Most of the points made above apply equally to 35mm slides. A few other ideas to bear in mind are:

— As the room is normally darkened, subtler colour contrasts can be used than with overhead transparencies, and reverse-image techniques (white or a pale colour on a dark background) are particularly powerful.

— Photographs can work very well, especially if interspersed with other graphics.

— Overlay techniques can be simulated by using a sequence of successively more complete slides, building up to the whole.

Slides are potentially a very dramatic medium. To exploit this, the narrative needs to be carefully and vividly scripted in *spoken* rather than written language – say it aloud to see how it sounds. Timing and pacing also make a great difference to the impact. Do not show a slide and talk about it for half a minute, then show the next and talk about that for half a minute, then show the next ... While an average of about half a minute's narrative per slide is about right, you may want to talk about one slide for three or four minutes, and then flip through the next six without saying anything.

As an addendum, direct computer projection of visual material is a similar technique to using slides. It is, however, much more versatile and impressive; you can change and create images on the spot, and you can even add animation and sound effects. Not surprisingly, it is *much* more expensive!

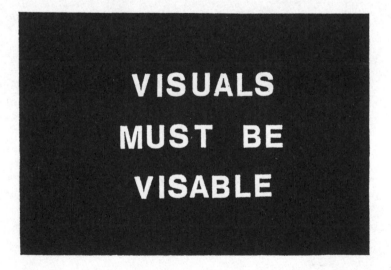

Figure 9.6 *35 mm slide*

I use Figure 9.6 in a short 35mm slide presentation on the use of visual aids. It makes these points:

- The ostensible message about visibility.
- The greater impact of the reverse-image presentation.
- The obvious importance of checking and proofreading.
- The uncomfortable fact that, the more professional the medium, the more glaring any error appears. The same spelling mistake, written on a flip chart in class, could be passed over with a joking correction. This cannot be done with a 35mm slide.

Not bad for four words.

Other Visual Aids

The main function of flip charts, whiteboards and blackboards is to allow the trainer to produce instant visual aids during the session. (Flip charts, of course, can also be used for ready-prepared material.) They *must* be legible, and it is harder to write neatly on boards than on a flip chart. Squared flip chart paper is a boon.

Posters are often the focal point for a lecture or discussion. They therefore need to be strongly designed to keep the audience's attention. *Remember the rules about simplicity, pictures and colour.* Posters are excellent for anything you want to keep up as a permanent reminder. They are also particularly suitable for mapping a process which you will be discussing in your training session. Incidentally, with a complex process chart, you may want to cover parts initially, and reveal them progressively as the session develops.

Preparing posters *can* be very time-consuming. But it need not be. The quickest way I know is to take an A4 master (for example, one prepared for an overhead transparency) and enlarge it to A3 or A2 size. You can then stick this onto coloured card to provide a frame. Very easy, very effective, and very cheap. And, as a final word, look after your posters. They are generally less durable than other visual aids, and so it makes sense to laminate them with clear plastic film, and arrange for protective storage.

Figure 9.7 *Poster prepared from A4 master*

10 Course Handouts

▷ SUMMARY ◁

Trainers can:

- Produce handout materials themselves.
- Let students take their own notes.
- Adopt a combination approach.

All these options have advantages and disadvantages, but the combination approach usually works best. An easy way to create such handouts is to base them on copies of the visuals, with space on the opposite page for student notes.

Three Options

Trainers have three options regarding course handouts: to provide reference information for students, to let students take their own notes, or to use a combination approach.

Ready-made Handouts

After the excitement of thinking through and preparing the course content, many trainers find handouts boring to write. It is hardly surprising, therefore, that many students find them boring to read, and frequently do not bother to do so. To avoid having this happen with your handouts:

- Remember KISS. Only include *necessary* information, for your students' sake and your own; structure the information so that students can use and refer to it easily; do not forget the headings; write short paragraphs, short sentences, short words; use a lively, direct style.
- Use acronyms (eg KISS = Keep It Short and Simple, PUP = Please Use Pictures) to help students remember key points.
- Remember PUP. Pictures, including charts, line drawings or photographs (just make sure they can be clearly reproduced) enliven and clarify text. They should not be an add-on, but an integral and fundamental part of the handout.
- Use layout to attract and retain attention.
- Consider using other formats than A4 sheets, eg A5 checklists for personal filing systems, reminder cards which fit into a diary or pocket, laminated posters to stick above the workplace. Your aim is not a row of glossy training manuals sitting on the shelf, unopened and unread.

Advantages of trainer-produced handouts are:

- You can make sure they are complete and accurate.
- Students can spend their training time *learning*, rather than just noting down your words.

Disadvantages are:

- It is difficult to find the right time to distribute handouts. **Before the event**, some people may read them in advance, but others (usually the less able or knowledgeable) will not, causing even greater disparity in students' starting knowledge. Also, some people may actually see the handout as a substitute for the training session and not attend at all. **During the session**, the temptation is to read them at that stage instead of concentrating on the presentation. **After the event**, you are most likely to have students file-and-forget them.
- Participants may 'switch off' and concentrate less, when they know there is a handout covering the topic.
- Given that individual students inevitably have different needs, none of the information you provide will be useful for everybody. Finding relevant needles in a pile of hay is rarely worth much effort – and that is what it may feel like to the student. This is the biggest reason why training handouts are largely ignored back on the job.

Do-It-Yourself

This is the reverse of having the trainer provide ready-made handouts.

The big advantage of having students take their own notes is not that it saves you time and effort (although, of course, it does), but that the notes are more personal to the student and may consequently be better used after the training.

The main disadvantage is that the student who is busy scribbling has the time neither to listen, nor to think, nor to ask questions – a total waste of face-to-face training. Also the notes may be incomplete. This is not always a problem: indeed it is an advantage, if the exclusions are deliberate omissions of less relevant points. But they are more likely to occur because of chance, lack of concentration, or the difficulty of writing at speaking-speed.

Combination Approach

Here the trainer provides an outline of the main points covered, with space for the students to amplify as they please.

The outlines should be more than just topic headings. Set out important rules and checklists in full. Use diagrams and pictures to clarify the material and aid retention. Either include all necessary reference material or make sure the students can get hold of it easily. And invite the students to note examples from their own experience to which the training points might be applied. However, do beware of putting in so much information that the outline becomes (and is treated as) trainer-produced notes.

If you use overhead transparencies, slides or prepared flip chart sheets to reinforce your main training points, you can include copies of these in the outline. One easy approach is to have a photocopy of the visuals on the left-hand pages, with space for additional notes on the facing right-hand pages. These right-hand pages should consist of the outline guide with sufficiently large gaps for the students' comments. In an emergency, however, they can be left blank, with the visual copies then providing the total trainer input to the handout.

If you are using a combination approach, you need to pay particular attention to format and presentation. You will add considerably to the professional image if you have a border on your pages. This is not difficult – a master can be produced manually or with a computer package, and copied.

Workbooks (bound or stapled) or loose-leaf folders are more practical than loose sheets stapled together. Not only are they less likely to get lost, but they can be opened flat to let the student see both left and right-hand pages.

You may also want to include any exercises or case study briefings in the workbooks rather than handing them out separately. This certainly looks tidier, but do consider very carefully how the exercise will be performed. With some exercises, it would be extremely awkward to have to carry about a workbook or training manual. With others you may not want the participants reading the exercise before you get to it.

In general, the combined approach tries to provide the best of both worlds — the completeness and accuracy of trainer-produced notes, made more relevant and personal by the student's involvement.

Its biggest disadvantage is that it may restrict the flexibility of the training session. Students will expect the trainer to cover all the points in the workbook in order, whereas, for that particular group, the trainer may wish to reverse the order or concentrate on some aspects rather than others. You can still do this, of course, provided that you explain to the students when you are deviating, and that you know your workbook well enough to direct them to the right page.

Figure 10.1 *Combination approach course manual*

11 Course Exercises

▷ SUMMARY ◁

Exercises need as much preparation as any other part of the training course. There are five main stages in preparing all exercises:

- Identify exercise objective
- Outline problem
- Devise solution

- Prepare instructions for student and trainer
- Dry run

Major types of exercises include:

- Case studies
- Role plays
- Games

- Mazes
- In-basket exercises

The Easy Option?

An exercise can seem an easy, not to say lazy, way of filling a slack half-hour or more on a training course – set the participants a problem, the more open-ended the better, and let them get on with it – minimal preparation and a welcome breathing space for the trainer. Ideal, one might think, but the reality is very different. Exercises often take *more* preparation than any other part of the teaching plan, and the success of the outcome may depend on how carefully they are written. Running the exercise, too, may be very taxing for the trainer. Like all forms of student involvement, exercises can have unexpected results. We have all experienced the role play which goes awry, or the pre-course test which suggests that the students already know as much as the trainer! But even if they are not always an easy option, exercises are a very valuable one – they create participation and increase learning dramatically.

The same principles apply whatever kind of exercise you are writing. The basic approach has five stages.

Identify Objective

What teaching points is the exercise intended to make? What kind of learning is sought:

- Memorization (of facts or processes)?
- Understanding (of principles and situations)?
- Performance (of actions)?

How do these aspects integrate with the rest of the course?

Outline Problem

There are two elements here: choosing a question, example or situation, and describing it.

The example should be one familiar to all participants, and the choice should therefore be determined by what you know about the participants.

Describing the problem is the core of the exercise. Consider carefully how much information to include – too little, and the students have to make assumptions, which increases the number of possible solutions; too much, and either the example becomes so complex that students get confused, or the solution becomes too obvious and easy. However, it is worth bearing in mind that what may seem too much information from your point of view, as creator of the exercise, may be too little for the student who comes to it cold.

Devise Solution

Where there is a single correct solution, explain it as simply as possible and, if helpful, the method of reaching it.

Where there is no 'right' answer, say so and offer a 'suggested' solution, possibly identifying where this falls short of the ideal. You may want to offer alternative solutions, emphasizing their comparative good and bad points, but take care not to over-complicate the exercise.

Even if the solution will not be handed out to the students, it should still be written. This ensures consistency when different trainers run the exercise.

Prepare Instructions

These are instructions both for the student, on how to complete the exercise, and for the trainer, on how to run it. They must be clear and straightforward.

The trainer's instructions should be detailed enough to allow another trainer to run the exercise with minimal rehearsal. A standard format trainer's guide is useful to ensure that nothing essential is forgotten.

TRAINER'S GUIDE TO EXERCISE

Exercise: Course:
Format: Indiv/Pairs/Trios/Small gps/Whole gp
Duration: Location:
Other materials/equipment req:

Primary objective:

Other objectives:

Preparation:

Running the exercise:

Potential problems:

Figure 11.1 *Trainer's guide*

Dry Run Exercise

This is *essential*. The closer the test group is to the target group the better, but even if that is impossible, dry run the exercise on *someone*. It is amazing how often an exercise which looks perfectly reasonable on paper just does not work in practice. You are testing:

- *How well the exercise achieves its objective.*
- How easily the student can follow your instructions.
- How easily the student can complete the exercise.
- How good the solution is.
- The completeness of the trainer's guide.
- The timing, and possibly the location.

Case Studies

A case study is a description of a real or realistic situation which the students have to handle.

Case studies may be long (20 pages or more) or short (under half a page), but realism is always the key note. Problems may arise in choosing a situation to which all participants can relate. This is usually resolved by giving very detailed preliminary information, describing the situation and how it developed. Unfortunately, this can be so long and off-putting that participants at best just scan it. The amount of detail may be unavoidable. If so, pay particular attention to:

- Structure. Mention a topic in a single place only. Use headings to enable the student to refer back easily, even when developing the story line.
- Language. KISS, first and foremost. Then, consider that you are telling a tale. Novels often consist of at least one third dialogue to two thirds narrative. A case study may not be a novel, but conversation is an excellent way of 'lightening' the information and conveying emotion and personality. (Much more effective than writing: 'Mr Smith was angry.')
- Layout. Use white space to make the writing attractive, and ensure that reference information (eg organization charts, timetables, financial projections, etc) is easily found.

It is also a good idea to present as much as possible of the background information orally and visually (tell the group the basic situation, display photographs of the main protagonists etc) before handing out the case study.

Since time spent understanding the background is largely wasted time (from a training point of view), it is worth only wasting it once. Have all case studies and role plays on a course relate to the same situation. This also adds to the continuity of the course, providing a link between the various sections.

You can buy books of non-copyright case studies. These can, however, be unnecessarily long and complex, and so, rather than using them as they are, adapt them to *your* purpose.

Do remember, too, that short case studies can provide just as rich a learning experience as long ones. The alternative to lengthy background information is a situation which all participants can recognize at once. For example, Figure 11.2 shows a favourite case study of mine.

You are manager of a department. A subordinate has BO (body odour). You have noticed it yourself on several occasions, but said nothing hoping the problem would disappear. Now another subordinate has complained to you and asked you to do something about it. How would you handle the situation?

Figure 11.2 *Short case study*

Role Plays

These may follow a case study discussion (for instance, the BO situation above), form part of a wider simulation (like a management game), or simply be introduced to enable students to practise particular communication skills.

They are often disliked by participants, who may feel nervous of exposing themselves, or consider the situation unreal and mere 'play-acting'. This unfortunately can get in the way of real learning, with participants reluctant to see any validity in the exercise. 'I wouldn't behave like that if I wasn't nervous / if it was a real situation' is a common disclaimer. There are several ways of opposing this usually erroneous view.

First, the trainer can, when introducing the exercise, point out that:

- Role plays are a concentrated experience, and most people therefore demonstrate a stronger, more concentrated version of their normal behaviour.
- This is the value of role plays, as this concentrated behaviour is more obvious and therefore easier to analyse than 'real life'

95

behaviour. It is not, however, fundamentally any different from 'real life' behaviour, just less dilute.

The trainer should also stress that role plays are not intended as 'get-it-right' exercises, but are an opportunity to try out new forms of behaviour and learn from these, and should handle the debrief from this standpoint.

Second, the better the background briefing, the more comfortable most students feel with the exercise. This is a big advantage of linking role plays to a case study situation. Another way of increasing the realism of role plays is to base them on a real-life situation encountered by the participants.

Games

Games are also often referred to as 'simulations' or 'activities', although distinctions may be drawn between these. However the term 'games' and in particular 'management games' is commonly used.

Games are long or short experiences, where the participants not only decide what to do about a situation (as in a case study, for instance), but also have to handle the results of their decisions.

Many games and activities are available commercially, and I would suggest using a ready-made game rather than writing your own, provided, of course, that it fits your requirements reasonably well. Writing games is much more complicated than writing case studies. However, commercially available games are written to cater for very general needs which may not match your particular situation. In that case, you may decide to devise your own.

Points to note when writing text-based games include:

- Depending on the skills being practised, the situation chosen may be less 'realistic' than for a case study. In the conventions of a management game, it is acceptable to choose situations which invite participants to suspend disbelief, such as crossing a desert or running a political election. However the problem and solution must be internally consistent and they should stick to their own rules. If a 'realistic' situation is chosen (as is necessary for technical simulations and may be preferable for some management ones), it needs to be *very* realistic.
- Professional presentation of the materials (eg robust, laminated boards or cards) is critical. It encourages the participants to take the scenario seriously and thus aids the suspension of disbelief; it also lengthens the life of frequently used materials.

– *Test, test, test,* not once but many times. Games are complex exercises and you are unlikely to be able to predict all reactions and outcomes. However the more you try out the game, the more likely you are to discover what can go wrong and what to do about it.

– Include full trainer's notes, and, if appropriate, a model solution. This should be presented in photocopiable form, as you are likely to want to hand it out to participants.

Mazes

These are also extensions of the case study, and may be considered as individual games. Typically a situation is described, and a problem posed with a choice of three or four solutions. According to the solution chosen, the student is directed to different pages in the exercise. One solution is correct, or at least preferred; in the response, explain *why* it is 'right', however – the student may have picked it by chance or may not have been certain of the answer. Similarly, in the responses to the 'wrong' solutions, explain the reasons for not choosing them, and direct the student either back to the initial problem or on to the next stage of the exercise.

An alternative way of handling 'wrong' responses is to develop these situations too, creating different problems with exponentially-multiplying outcomes. Clearly there is a limit to the number of stages which you can introduce without burying the student in paper.

With mazes take care to:

– Keep the situation at the right level of complexity as it develops through the various stages.
– Choose responses which are *all* realistic.

John finally emerges from his meeting and goes back to his desk. He looks at the mountain of paper in his in-tray. It is 6.30 pm and he is exhausted. Should he:

(a) Make a start on it now?

(b) Give up and go home?

(c) Plan tomorrow's activities?

– respond to the 'right' solution with brief, non-patronizing, non-repetitive praise. Identify any disadvantages of the 'right' solution (as well, of course, as the advantages):

You thought John should give up and go home.

You are right.

John started his day early and he has not stopped rushing from one task to another. He badly needs to plan tomorrow's activities to avoid a repeat of today, but not now. Tomorrow morning he will feel fresher and will prioritize better.

- Respond carefully to the 'wrong' solutions, so as not to discourage students. Identify any advantages of the 'wrong' solutions (as well as the disadvantages):

You thought John should plan tomorrow's activities.

I don't agree.

You are right in saying that he badly needs to establish his priorities and plan tomorrow's activities, but not now. He started his day early and has not stopped rushing from one task to another. He is exhausted and in no fit state to prioritize properly. Stress can be dangerous and John's most important need at the moment is to relax and go home.

- Make the link to the next problem a logical outcome of the solution.
- Offer a route map of 'right' answers for future reference.

In-basket Exercises

These are again individual exercises. Students receive a package of documents (letters, memos etc) which represent a typical in-basket and which they have to handle, usually within a strict time limit. Although commercial exercises exist, they are often less useful than trainer-written ones which reflect the students' own in-baskets. When writing these exercises:

- Make sure students know what they are expected to do. For example should they, in response to a particular document, just state that they would write a memo, or should they actually draft that memo?
- Include enough different documents to cause a variety of decisions to be made.
- Link some of the documents, so that a decision on one will have an impact on others.
- Ensure that the different documents reflect the different positions, perspectives and personalities of their supposed authors.

Figure 11.3 shows an example of an in-basket introduction and Figure 11.4 of a typical item.

IN-BASKET EXERCISE

You are John Baker, Office Services Manager.

A company organization chart and some additional information are attached to this exercise. The envelope clipped to the back of the exercise contains the contents of your in-basket.

It is Sunday 13 May, and you have just come back from three weeks' holiday. Dedication to duty (or a suspicion that there may be nasty surprises waiting for you) have prompted you to come into the office today to clear your in-basket. However, you do not want to spend more than half an hour on the task. A glance at your diary tells you that you have an appointment to see the Managing Director, Philip Smith, at 9.00 am on Monday morning. You have half an hour to go through your in-basket.

Note on each item how you would handle it. If you would speak to somebody about the item (either face-to-face or by phone), write down the gist of what you would say. If you would write to somebody about it, note briefly what you would write.

Figure 11.3 *In-basket introduction*

MEMORANDUM

To: J Baker   Date: 27 April
From: P Smith
Subject: Security

It has come to my attention that unlawful entries have been made by strangers found on our premises.

This week, as I assume you have been informed, one miscreant was apprehended during the lunch hour, walking out with a **personal computer.**

That such an appalling situation could ever occur leads me to believe that we are extremely lax in our security arrangements.

I wish to discuss with you **immediately you return from holiday** what action you propose taking to tighten security arrangements.

Figure 11.4 *In-basket item*

Other Exercises

Other written exercises can include tests and questionnaires (see Chapter 7). With all such exercises, ensure that the questions cover the most important points, by linking them directly with the exercise objectives.

There are a number of test formats:

— Multiple choice
If ..., would you (a) ... (b) ... or (c) ...?
Cynically called 'multiple guess' because of the, often high, possibility of students' choosing the right answer by chance, these are nevertheless extremely useful exercises. They are very flexible, quick to complete and simple to write and mark. Their validity increases if the 'wrong' answers (also known as 'distractors') are carefully chosen and phrased, such as in the maze exercise examples, above.

— Matching
Which of the following items are connected?

— Fill-in-the-blanks
Insert the correct term in the following sentence.

— True-or-false
Which of the following statements are correct?

— Sequencing
Put the following items in order.

Like multiple choice questions, these four types all mainly test discrimination and have limited validity. They too are quick and simple, but less flexible than multiple choice exercises.

— Essay or free response
Describe the relationship between...
Questions such as these are the only way of testing depth of knowledge and understanding, but they are hard to mark consistently. Model answers are a useful aid to consistent marking and also much appreciated by students.

12 Self-learning Texts

▷   SUMMARY   ◁

Self-learning texts are very different from textbooks. The emphasis is on *helping* the learner to learn. Important aspects to consider are:

- Having specific and detailed objectives.
- Using graphics for visual relief and signposting.
- Repeating information through summaries and checklists.
- Using other media if appropriate.
- Including exercises to give the learner practice.
- Including tests to identify how well the objectives have been achieved.
- Charting the complete self-learning package to show how sections interrelate.
- Providing study advice.
- Presenting the material in such a way as to encourage active participation.
- Dry running the material.

What Are Self-learning Texts?

These are any written materials designed to help an individual learn on his or her own.

There have always been textbooks, of course, but many textbooks are passive in purpose – they aim simply to make information available. 'Helping an individual learn' means involving the learner actively, for instance by completing exercises, answering test questions, and applying the information to on-the-job situations.

There are many self-learning materials available commercially. You can even subscribe to databases which guide the trainer in choosing the most appropriate materials. Commonly called 'open learning' or 'distance learning' materials, they are the new generation of 'correspondence courses' or 'programmed instruction'.

Why Should You Write Them?

If there is so much available, you may think, why should you ever need to produce self-learning texts yourself? The obvious answer is: if there is nothing which meets your learners' exact needs.

One important example of this is induction, both to the company (new employees) and to a new job (promotions, transfers). A new job is a major stress event in a person's life. It is also a major opportunity for the employer. New job-holders often feel vulnerable and insecure. Make them feel 'part of the team' and they will stay on your side for ever. Induction training, which helps them to settle in quickly and get to grips with their new jobs, boosts morale *and* productivity – surely it is the magic answer to many management problems. And yet induction training, when it is given at all, is usually haphazard, half-hearted, and weeks (or months) too late.

One of the main reasons for this is that new job-holders often are not 'they', several at a time, but more likely 'he' or 'she'. Self-learning materials are ideal for any training, which, like induction, has to be:

- Delivered promptly.
- Repeated frequently.
- Offered typically to few employees at any one time.
- Capable of being offered in different locations, maybe at the same time.

Objectives

There are several important elements to remember when writing self-learning materials. Objectives, of course, are critical for all writing, but with self-learning texts they need to be developed to a finer level of detail.

For example, for a handout on, say, house layout style, you might have an overall objective that readers should know and be able to apply the house rules. A self-learning text on the same topic would have several, more specific objectives. For instance:

After completing this material you will be able to:
- **Recognize our house layout style.**
- **Remember the different features of our house layout style.**
- **Identify which features are generally most important.**
- **Apply the house style to varied documents.**
- **In case of conflict, decide which features should be preferred, according to their relative importance and the document's purpose.**

Self-learning objectives should be spelled out clearly to the learners. This helps them map out where they are going and how much ground they have covered so far. Also, for some learners, to go back to our example, recognizing the house style might be enough for their needs; they would therefore only complete the first part of the material.

Text

The information-giving part. Again the principles are the same as for all writing. The normal question: 'How much information should you include?' is a key one; the answer is: 'Only as much as you need for the learner to achieve the objectives.' The more precise the objectives, the easier it is to write text.

In fact, actually *writing* the text may be best left until after you have written the tests (see below). This ensures a match between the tests and the information you have provided. On the other hand, writing in the order objectives-text-tests is more natural, and enables you to use the tests to double-check how appropriate and relevant both your objectives and text are.

Text should be written in easy-reading style – short and simple paragraphs, sentences and words. In particular make sure that each paragraph only makes one point. A number of single-sentence paragraphs are much better, in self-learning materials, than one or two more literary, longer ones. And bullet points or, even more useful, numbering help the learner identify the separate items.

Language and tone should be conversational, direct and friendly. Address the reader as 'you'; avoid jargon; use contractions ('don't' etc) and colloquial phrases (eg 'have a go at...'), although do be careful with anything too slangy. Such expressions date quickly and may offend some learners or be misunderstood by them.

Graphics

Also typical of self-learning materials is the use of graphics. Not just in illustration of points, although this is as important as with any other writing, but also:

- Graphic symbols, to indicate pictorially what the learner has to do next – an open book for 'read', a pen for 'write', a computer screen, video-tape, pair of headphones etc, as text is not the only way of giving information in self-learning packages.
- Cartoons and line drawings to inject humour and lighten the learning. You can normally use graphics produced for other purposes, eg course visuals, which can save you a lot of effort.

Summaries and Checklists

These help the learner by providing:

- A quick reference to what is covered.
- Repetition. The common summary-text-checklist pattern matches the old training adage, 'First you tell them what you're going to tell them, then you tell them, then you tell them what you told them.'
- Pauses for reflection, because summaries and checklists are in a different format from the main text, and this encourages a change of pace in the reader.

Other Media

As I mentioned, text is not the only way of giving information. Many commercial packages include computer-based, video or audio materials. However do not be seduced by this into thinking that *you* must include them too. Variation of media is certainly useful in maintaining the learner's interest, but only where the other media fulfil a purpose which text alone cannot achieve so well, such as showing actions or physical processes. You *can* produce computer, video and audio materials in-house, but:

- The very high quality of leisure products in these fields has given learners exceptionally high expectations. Amateur production may destroy the credibility, and hence effectiveness, of materials, however well designed they are from a training point of view.

- In particular, do not simply transfer written self-learning material on to a computer format, and consider that a computer-based training product. Using the computer as an 'electronic page turner' is justly condemned by professionals in this area. They are *different* media, and the computer has a lot more, and a lot less, to offer than a workbook.
- Commissioning professional production is very expensive for video, and to a lesser extent, audio and computer materials.
- Copyright restrictions affect just about *all* commercially available products, so do not try your hand at editing without having first obtained permission.

Exercises

As in face-to-face training, the aim is to provide the student with practice in demonstrating and applying the knowledge, understanding or skill which has been learnt. Many course exercises are perfectly suitable for self-learning.

Consider including case studies, individual games, mazes and in-baskets. Maze exercises are particularly useful; indeed these are fundamentally the same as 'programmed instruction', a long-established self-learning technique. There, an information block is followed by a multiple-choice question. 'Right' answers go on to the next information-block-plus-question; 'wrong' ones repeat the sequence or are directed to supplementary information.

Follow the basic approach outlined in Chapter 11, paying special attention to providing learners with feedback on their answers. As well as explaining what is 'right' or 'wrong', and why, you also need to offer the learner the 'personal' response which a course trainer would give. For example:

- **I agree. I think this would work extremely well ...**
- **This is a difficult problem. I would have tackled it this way.**
- **Oops! Have you forgotten about ..?**

It is important to:

- Vary your comments. Twenty repetitions of **Well done! Quite right!** or **Sorry, think again about this one** sound, and are, mechanistic, not personal.
- Avoid sounding patronizing. This is difficult, especially as you are constantly trying to vary your wording. The best advice is to think of the learner as an intelligent friend. What would you *say* to him or her?

Tests

Tests are, of course, exercises too. The most common formats are:

- Open questions and correct/model answers.
- Multiple choice questions.
- Matching.
- Fill-in-the-blanks.
- True-or-false.
- Sequencing.

The points made in Chapter 11 and above, all apply when writing tests for self-learning materials.

All exercises test a learner's knowledge to a greater or lesser extent. However, I have distinguished formal tests from other exercises, because their primary purpose is to identify to the learner how well the learning objectives have been achieved. Therefore you *must* ensure that your tests match your objectives and content.

One way of doing this is to write the tests as soon as you have prepared the objectives, and then write the text to match the tests. Another way, if you prefer to write the tests last, is to link particular test questions with particular objectives and information blocks. This way you can check if anything is missing, or has been given too much or too little emphasis.

And one trap which is often all too tempting, make sure your test questions cover the *critical* areas of knowledge, rather than simply those which are easy to assess.

Study Aids

A distinguishing feature of self-learning materials is the 'help the learner to learn' approach. Deliberate attention is paid, not just to the subject of the materials, but also to how the student can get the most out of them.

An especially useful aid is the flowchart or graphic representation of the complete self-learning package. This may show, for instance, which sections interrelate, key objectives for each session, and what activities the learner should perform. These may be an addition or an alternative to standard contents lists and indexes.

A second important study aid consists of advice on how to tackle the learning task. This may include hints on:

- Scheduling priorities.
- Selecting a convenient time and place for study.
- Organizing the material.
- Using reference documents, both external to the materials, eg a Thesaurus, and within the materials, eg an index or a glossary.
- Reading attentively.
- Writing answers.
- Remembering information.
- Applying it to the learner's job.
- Preparing for exams.

This advice may be concentrated at the beginning of the material, scattered throughout, or both.

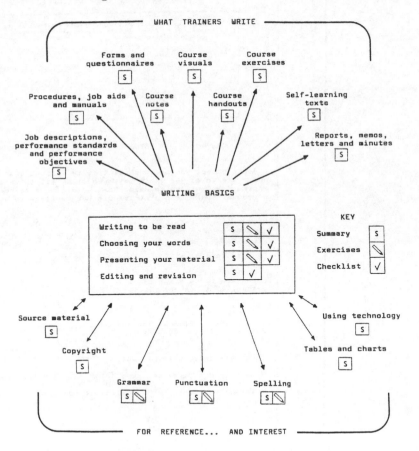

Figure 12.1 *Study chart for this book*

What Self-learning Texts Look Like

This is certainly the most *obvious* feature of self-learning materials, the appearance of the page. It is immensely important, and probably the greatest influence on whether people actually *complete* the self-learning text or merely skim through it.

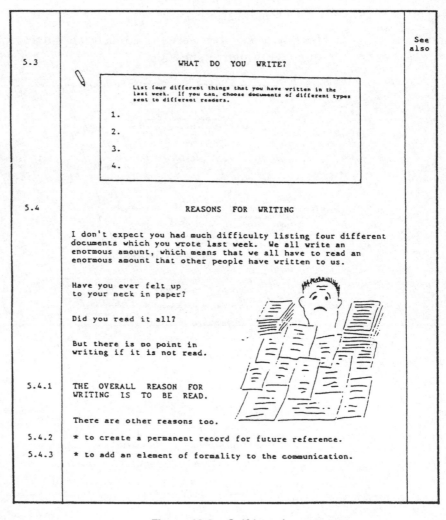

Figure 12.2 *Self-learning text page*

Some characteristics you can see on this page are:

- Distinct layout. White space, indentation, different length lines. Boxing round the exercises and different sized print highlight the change of activity. Different box designs can also be used to distinguish different types of activities.
- Making the structure obvious. The columns for section numbers and cross-references would be a standard throughout the self-learning text. Standard heading formats are used for each section.
- Graphics. Charts, graphic symbols and cartoon drawings.

This page has been produced using ordinary typing and photo-reduction, plus physical cut and paste. This is probably a sufficiently professional presentation for an in-house self-learning text, but proper printing or desk-top publishing (see Chapter 20) can make a great difference.

Dry Running the Material

Like all courses, self-learning texts *must* be dry run on potential users before being finalized. This can pose a problem regarding timing. Do you dry run your material before or after it has been printed? Since the appearance of the material is so significant, it is less useful to dry run before printing; on the other hand, reprinting because of changes is very expensive. This is fortunately becoming less of a problem with wider use of desk-top publishing.

13 Reports, Letters, Memos and Minutes

▷   SUMMARY   ◁

For completeness, this chapter looks at the standard writing tasks which trainers also need to perform, eg reports, letters, memos and minutes of meetings. As these are discussed in many other books, I will not cover them in any detail.

- Reports are most effective when written with the reader clearly in mind. SOPORRA (Summary – Objective – Position – Options – Recommendation – Required Action – Appendices) is a useful structure.
- Letters need to combine effectiveness with a polite, personal approach. The structure SCRAP (Situation – Complication – Resolution – Action – Politeness) helps to achieve this.
- Memos may be mini-reports or internal letters. Consider first whether they need to be written at all.
- Minutes should be written in a format which identifies actions to be implemented. They may be written during the meeting itself.

Reports

Reports are rarely popular. They are often too long (which makes them a chore both to write and read); they are written in a formal, indirect style (which is meant to impress, but doesn't); and they frequently fail to achieve their objectives.

Unfortunately, trainers may not be able to avoid writing reports. The UK *National Standards for Training and Development* refer to many different proposals that trainers should make, for instance proposals which identify:

    – The strategic contribution of training.
    – Human resource needs to carry out the strategy.
    – Training needs for those human resources.
    – Training resource needs to carry out the training.

And that is only in section A1! How do you submit all these proposals? Usually, as reports.

The main problem with reports is that they are often written to boards and committees – in other words to a number of people, some (even many) of whom the writer may not know. In trying to play safe and cover all contingencies, the report only serves as a graveyard for the good ideas buried inside. The points made in Chapter 1, about getting to know your readers and identifying their needs, are critical. If different readers may have conflicting needs, focus on those of the most influential reader (who is not always the most senior one).

    – What does he or she already know about the subject? (Don't repeat it.)
    – What are likely to be his or her concerns? (Treat them seriously.)
    – Priorities? (Reflect them in your arguments.)
    – Prejudices? (Either pander to them, or refute them with unemotional, non-critical logic.)

It is easier to keep reports short and to the point if you follow a set structure. SOPORRA (I hate to suggest it as a mnemonic as the last thing you want your reports to be is soporific!) stands for:

S ummary
O bjective
P osition
O ptions
R ecommendations
R equired action
A ppendices

A **summary** is only needed for reports of 4-5 pages or more. It should be no more than 10 per cent of the length of the whole report, ie summarize 4-5 pages in half a page maximum, 9-10 pages in one page maximum. (And try to keep the report to 10 pages at most!) Although it is often easiest to write the summary after the bulk of the report, it is very helpful to busy readers to find it on the front page, where it can be scanned quickly as soon as the report is picked up. Carefully-bound reports, with title and contents sheets and the summary buried on page 2 or 3, look attractive, but are less in tune with the reader's needs, and often get pushed to the bottom of the pile 'until there is time to read them'.

The **objective** (scope, terms of reference, etc) should be stated briefly to ensure that your readers do not have the wrong expectations. For example:

> **In this report, I recommend measures for training supervisors. I will consider management training separately in a later report.**

Next outline the current **position**. This may include some background information, but only if it is necessary to enable your readers to understand your recommendations, and only if they do not already know it.

If it is important to show that you have not skimped your research, mention briefly the various **options** you considered and discarded, and then home in on your chosen **recommendations**, giving your conclusions, the reasons for your choice, likely outcomes, timescales and costs.

Many reports reach this point, but then founder and achieve nothing. This may be because the report itself has not specified what **required action** should now be taken, by whom and by when. Spelling this out will make it more likely that your recommendations will be implemented, or, if they are rejected, may give you an opportunity to revise and resubmit your proposals.

Appendices should contain all the information the reader *needs* to know but which is too detailed to be included in the body of the report. Present calculations and statistical charts and tables as an appendix. Do not feel, however, that you *must* have appendices, and put in masses of merely 'nice to know' information, just to impress your readers. It will, on the contrary, only irritate them.

The different sections of a report should be identified with separate headings and sub-headings. This makes the argument clearer for the reader and allows easy reference to other sections. It is similarly often helpful to number sections and sub-sections.

Letters

Business letters should be polite, personal and effective. They should achieve your objective and enhance your relationship with your reader.

The first difficulty often comes right at the beginning. What do you call your reader?

Dear Mike or **Dear Mary** is suitable if you know the person well enough, and if the informality is appropriate to the tone and content of your letter.

Dear Mr Smith may seem safe in response to a letter signed 'M Smith', but it will hardly enhance your relationship with Mary Smith, let alone Dr Smith or Professor Smith. Getting someone's name wrong is a fundamental insult. It is worth a few minutes' research (check previous correspondence, ask colleagues, even telephone M Smith's secretary) to avoid this sort of mistake.

If you do not know whether the woman to whom you are writing is married, you have the choice of:

- **Dear Miss Smith** (This used to be conventional; it is much less acceptable these days.)
- **Dear Ms Smith** (Many people hate it, but it *is* convenient.)
- **Dear Mary Smith** (Personally, I always think this reads oddly, but it is an alternative to 'Ms' which is gaining in popularity.)
- **Dear Madam** (This sounds stilted and formal.)

If you do not know your reader's name, **Dear Sir** or **Dear Madam** is conventional. **Dear Sir or Madam** sounds like a government circular.

The beginnings of letters are prone to 'commercialese'.

With regard to your esteemed favour of 14th inst may be moribund, but it is all too often replaced with: **Re your letter dated ...**

Thank you for your letter of ... is polite and avoids a sentence structure which can otherwise sometimes be tortuous.

It is a good idea to start a letter with a heading giving the subject of the letter – this concentrates the reader's mind and aids efficient filing. Incidentally, there is no reason why longer business letters, covering several points, should not include sub-headings or section numbers. As in reports, these add clarity to the structure.

A well-known mnemonic for structuring letters is SCRAP.

S ituation
C omplication
R esolution or recommendation
A ction
P oliteness

In the **situation**, outline or refer to what has happened so far, but do not dwell on anything your reader already knows. The **complication** is what is actually causing you to write the letter.

The **resolution or recommendation** should be expressed from the reader's point of view. Writing 'you' as much as possible will make your arguments more persuasive – **You will benefit from this by ...** rather than: **I recommend this because ...** And the **action** (who, how, where, when) makes the recommendation specific.

The **politeness** or ending may again pose problems. It is sometimes difficult to steer between the weak or meaningless: **I look forward to hearing from you,** and the sometimes abrupt or aggressive: **Unless I hear from you by next Monday, I shall ...** Write your ending to suit your reader, but in general the more positive and specific your choice of words, the more likely you are to achieve your objective.

The final salutation should match the initial form of address:

- **Dear (name) ... Yours sincerely.**
- **Dear Sir ... Yours faithfully.**

And to save your reader problems when replying to your letter, include with your name any particular form of address you prefer (eg Miss, Mrs, Ms, Dr etc).

Memos

Memos are usually written in response to memos received; they themselves often generate further memos in reply, which in turn ... Think very carefully before writing a memo. Is it necessary? Would a telephone call serve your purpose better? Can you reply in a few words handwritten on the original?

Memos may be mini-reports, or letters sent to colleagues within your organization. Follow whichever guidelines seem appropriate, and your house style regarding salutation and signature. This may range from omitting both (the sender's and receiver's names merely being typed at the top of the memo), to inserting a handwritten **Dear John** at the beginning of the memo and **Cordially, Bill** at the end. This second approach is more typical of US than British organizations.

Minutes

Minutes are a formal record of all points discussed or decided in a meeting. That does not imply that they can or should be a verbatim transcript of all that was said. They are a factual summary, and one of their most important practical functions is to ensure that all actions agreed by the meeting are implemented. A simple format can help this to happen.

Training Committee Meeting   Date: 31 October 1990

Those present: P Thomson (Chairman)
                J Soames
                M Johnson
                L Edwards

Agenda item	Discussion/Action	Who?	When?
1	Time management course. All agreed need was clearly established. JS considered 3 days too long. 2-day course:		
	– to be prepared and dry run	MJ	By end Dec 90
	– pilot run for Marketing Div	MJ	By end Mar 91

Figure 13.1 *Meeting minutes*

Such brief minutes can actually be written during the meeting, copied and handed to participants at the end. This obviously encourages action to be taken promptly, but it has another advantage. By summarizing each major discussion point briefly to the meeting and then recording it, the minute-writer both contributes to the efficient conduct of the meeting, and ensures that the minutes are correct and agreed at the time.

Part 3 For Reference . . .
and Interest

14 Source Material

▷   SUMMARY   ◁

The two main sources of training material are people and documents.
- 'People' sources include company colleagues, training course participants, professional colleagues outside your company and librarians or information assistants. Confidentiality must be observed when using real experiences.
- Information from people is usually written down at some stage and becomes a 'paper' source. Other 'paper' sources include books, magazines, company documents, training materials already written (by yourself or others), publicity material about external courses and products etc. The US Armed Service Technical Information Agency documentation system allows quick and easy filing and retrieval of this mass of information.

Sources

Every trainer needs to use other sources in order to get ideas and information for training materials. This can be a rather haphazard process:

Now, wasn't I speaking to someone about that recently? Was it at the training association branch meeting, or at that film launch, or at the exhibition last month ...? And who was it, anyway?

I'm sure I read an article about that. Where can it be?

119

Sources generally come in two shapes – people and paper. This chapter will cover methods of organizing your source materials for easy retrieval.

People

All writers use other people as sources for what they write, and trainers are no different in this from any group of writers. 'People' sources for trainers include colleagues (both inside and outside the organization), trainees and official information-givers (librarians, etc).

Most trainers try to pick the brains of managers in their company to get information for teaching points, exercises, case studies etc. This is intended to give their material the 'real-life' validity which trainees seek, and which helps convince management of the relevance of the training. Unfortunately, much of this 'company background' is (and appears to be) a superficial gloss rather than fundamental to the material. This is often because the use of this company information is unplanned and comes too late in the course design process. As well as pre- and post-course discussions with participants' managers, the best time to collect this sort of information is when initially discussing training needs – all those grumbles about what people can't do should not only govern the training objectives, but can also provide many specific examples to use within the material. Remembering these examples, of course, can be a problem, so don't – write them down and file them as suggested below, and then you will have them easily accessible to use from the earliest stage of the course design.

An important point to consider is confidentiality, but usually false names and discreet changes of department or background are enough to protect the protagonists. However do not be surprised if your trainees know more than you do about the situation, or think they do. I once used a case study about a manager with a 'drink problem'. I camouflaged his identity very successfully, only to have the trainees identify the character as somebody else!

Training course participants themselves are obviously another excellent source of material. Asking them, before the course, to choose and be prepared to discuss four or five relevant situations which they have experienced, makes their contributions richer and more varied. Confidentiality is again paramount, both from yourself and from the other course members. It may be that some of these experiences provide such powerful learning material that you would like to use them on other courses – this *must* only be with the participant's permission and with any identifying details altered, otherwise you risk losing your trainees' trust.

Confidentiality is less of a problem with situations related by colleagues outside your company. In order to milk this rich information source fully, a little organization and a card case are required. Exchange business cards with external colleagues, and do not just thrust the card in your pocket and forget about it. When turning out your pockets that evening, note on the back of the card when and where you met the person and the main topics you talked about, and then keep the card in your card case. The frustration saved is more than worth the effort.

And don't forget the 'official' sources of material. Information services, professional or management organizations, libraries are all there to help you, so use them. Appendix 2 lists a number of organizations I use, but you may want to compile your own list (add contact names wherever you can) and keep it handy for reference.

Paper

In order to avoid having to remember, and forgetting, all the information you glean from these 'people' sources, you need to write it down and be able to find it again when you want it. The same is true of all your other 'paper' sources of material:

- Books and magazines.
- Company documents (procedures, forms, reports, etc) both from your current company and previous ones.
- Training courses (lesson plans, handouts, etc), your own and those other people have given you, current courses and old ones.
- Publicity information (covering external courses, training films, generic training materials, etc).

Over a number of years this adds up to a huge pile of paper.
You need a filing system that enables you to:

- Identify instantly whether you have any information on a given subject.
- Retrieve, in minutes, all the information you have on that subject.
- Even, find an article you read five years ago and had forgotten about, but which is just what you need now.

121

The simplicity of the US Armed Service Technical Information Agency Uniterm System for Coordinate Indexing belies the complexity of its name. Once the system has been set up, filing documents is straightforward and retrieving them unbelievably easy. (If I sound enthusiastic, I am.)

To start the system, take any document you want to keep. Give it a number – start with 1 and continue in strict numerical order – and write the number actually on the document. Then consider what the document is about. Jot down all the key words that describe for you what that document covers, again either on the front of the document or on a piece of paper stapled to it, if that is more convenient. For instance a handout for a writing skills course might have 'TRAINING', 'HANDOUT' and 'WRITING' as key words. These are the classifications by which the document will be filed and retrieved.

These key words, and those for all the other documents you wish to keep, are the basis of the filing system. You may think that you would have an infinite number of key words, but in fact the same ones will crop up repeatedly, reflecting your interests and concerns. In a fully developed system about 500 – 1000 key words are normally used. The filing system may be organized manually, with index cards, or on a computer. You have one card or record per key word, and on it you list all the document numbers of documents with this key word. You also need alphabetical index cards or records, listing all your key words for that letter. And that is the whole system.

WRITING			
36	261	400	693
102	267	428	
151	299	500	
	352	516	
		517	
		520	

Figure 14.1 *Key word card*

A

ABILITIES	ALCOHOL	ASSERTIVENESS
ABSENCE	ANALYSIS	ASSESSMENT
ACCOUNTABILITY	APPLICATION	ATTITUDE
ACTION	APPRAISAL	AUDIO
ADMINISTRATION	APPROVAL	AUDIT
AGE	ARCHETYPES	AUXILIARY
AIDS	ARTICLES	

Figure 14.2 *Alphabetical key word list*

To file a document, write its number and key words on the document itself and record its number on all the appropriate key word cards. If you need to create a new key word card, do so, simply adding it to the alphabetical list. Physically file the documents themselves in numerical order.

To retrieve a document, consult the alphabetical list to see if you have filed any documents for the key words you want. It does help to avoid synonyms – for instance, do not have both 'AIM' and 'OBJECTIVE' as key words, but choose one and stick to it. If the word is listed, the key word card will give you the numbers of all the documents on that topic. Now you may not want *all* the documents associated with a particular key word, so you can combine the key word cards to narrow your choice. When you are hunting for a Writing Skills course handout, 'TRAINING' might produce a list of, say, 200 documents, but only 20 of those numbers appear also on the 'WRITING' card and only 2 of these on the 'HANDOUT' card – a manageable number.

Date key words (eg '1991') are useful if you want to weed your filing system periodically. You probably will not want to do that with all documents but some, eg publicity material, may only have a short-term relevance. In that situation, include the date when you want to review or discard the material as an additional key word. At the end of the period, you can retrieve all dated material and decide whether or not to keep it. If you want to discard it, throw it away and cross the document number off all the associated key word cards. (You know what they are as they are written on the front of the document.)

This system takes a little time to set up, but once in use it is simple and foolproof.

15 Copyright

▷   **SUMMARY**   ◁

When using outside source materials you may well have to consider the question of copyright.
This chapter looks at:

- What copyright is.
- What works are subject to copyright.
- How long it lasts.
- What constitutes breaches of copyright.
- Exceptions to these.

If you want to use a work which is protected by copyright, you either need to seek permission from the copyright owner, or reword and develop the ideas for yourself, relating them to your own organization.

Disclaimer

I want to start this chapter with a disclaimer. I am not a lawyer and I do not pretend to give legal advice. I am simply setting out here the broad principles behind UK copyright law (these are very similar in most other countries), and indicating in very general terms whether a work is likely to be subject to copyright, and what to do about it.

However, copyright legislation is extremely complex. *If you have any specific concerns, check with a lawyer who specializes in this area.* Lawyers' fees are cheaper than damages!

What Is Copyright?

Copyright is a right, which entitles the owner of an original, created work to prevent other people from copying or publishing that work, or a substantial part of it, for a certain period of time.

'Work' covers, among others, literary, artistic, dramatic and musical works. It includes sound recordings, films and computer programmes. The most important works from the point of view of the trainer are:

- Written works. 'Literary', the term used in the legislation, is a catch-all phrase which does not imply artistic merit. Memos and letters are 'literary' works; so are tables of numbers and computer programmes; so, of course, are published books and articles. Charts, plans, sketches, photographs, etc are also subject to copyright, but they are classed as 'artistic' works.
- Videos, films, audio cassettes.

'Copying' means, very roughly, any form of reproduction, whether or not the copy is shown to other people. The reproduction has to be of the *form* of the work – the actual words which were written, the pictures, the film, etc, and *not just* the ideas which those words, pictures or film express.

'Publishing' means distributing, performing or making available to other people.

The restricted period of time is, most commonly:

- for written work, 50 years after the death of the creator of the work.
- for videos etc, 50 years after the work was first registered or shown.

These are gross simplifications. Copyright law is a minefield, with a number of successive Acts each adding its quota of amendments, additions and exceptions. The Copyright, Designs and Patents Act 1988 aims to simplify the situation, and cover all eventualities under one comprehensive, consistent umbrella.

However, a number of provisions under the older Acts still apply. As I said, if in doubt, consult a lawyer.

What Works Are Protected by Copyright?

There are two principal factors to consider: time and place.

1 Time. Generally, written works are protected until 50 years after the year when their author died. (For joint authors, 50

125

years after the year of death of the last surviving author.) Works published posthumously before 1 August 1989, are protected for 50 years after the year of their first publication. This means that an eighteenth century work found and first published in 1991 would not be subject to copyright, but one first published in 1988 would be protected until the end of 2038.

Films, videos, and sound recordings are protected for fifty years after the year they were made *or* released, whichever is the longer.

If the copyright is owned by the Crown (see below), the work is protected for 125 years from when it was created, or 50 years from when it was first published, whichever is the longer.

2 Place. UK copyright law covers works by British citizens ('British' in its widest sense), and works published in the UK and certain other countries. However, international copyright conventions, which the UK has signed along with virtually every other country, mean that we offer the same protection to the works of 'foreign' nationals as we do to our own. (Similarly, UK copyright owners are protected overseas, although each country may have particular requirements, eg US copyright must be registered and, in the past, regularly reviewed.)

In general, assume that most material you will want to use is protected.

What Can You Not Do?

The 'restricted acts'. These are, of course, only restricted if they apply to a work protected by copyright. As far as the trainer is concerned, the main restricted acts are:

- Copying a work or a substantial part of one. This includes copying by hand, typing, photocopying, photographing, faxing, computer copying, filming, sound recording, video copying, audio cassette copying – in fact, assume it covers *any* form of copying.

    Exact copying, for instance photocopies, photographs or facsimile copies, may in addition infringe the copyright of the typographical layout owned by the publisher of the work.
- Issuing copies of the work, or playing or performing it in public.
- Adapting a work. This covers translations, and converting a work from one medium to another, for example writing the

story of a video and using it as a case study, or transferring text-based materials on to a computer.
- Importing, possessing, distributing or showing any copy of a work, which you have reason to believe was made in breach of copyright.

Exceptions

There are some situations in which a 'restricted act' may not infringe copyright. The important ones which might affect trainers are:

- Copying, quoting or publishing less than a 'substantial' part of the work. Unfortunately there is no definition of 'substantial' in the Act, each case being judged on its own merits. However it is not merely a matter of length; importance counts at least as much. And it may be considered that anything important enough to copy is important enough to protect.
- Research and private study. If you are preparing a training programme and need to research a particular aspect, you are entitled to make copies of works to help you in that research. However, that only applies to *your* research and private study; you may not share your copies with colleagues or students.
- Criticism and review. If you are criticizing or reviewing a work, you may reproduce parts of that work in your review, provided that you give 'sufficient acknowledgment', ie identify the work by author and title.
- Reading and recitation. These are permitted, provided that you make sufficient acknowledgement.
- Educational establishments. These are defined in the 1988 Act as schools and institutions for Higher and Further Education. Representatives of these establishments may copy material (except printed music) for examinations, and, subject to restrictions, for instruction. The instruction restrictions are that not more than 1 per cent of any work should be copied in any calendar quarter, unless the educational establishment has a licence which allows more extensive copying. Blanket licences exist, like the one issued by the Copyright Licensing Agency which covers all local authority schools.

   If you do not know whether you qualify as an educational establishment, or are covered by a licence, contact the National Council for Educational Technology (for address, see Appendix 2).

Permission to Copy or Publish

If you want to carry out a restricted act in respect of a work that is subject to copyright, you need to get permission from the copyright owner. This is initially the author or employer (if the work was produced by an employee during the course of employment). The Crown is the first owner of copyright of any work produced by an officer or servant of the Crown (including all government and civil service employees) during the course of his or her duties.

The ownership of copyright may be assigned permanently to another person or a temporary licence may be given. In seeking permission to copy or publish material, contact the current owner (author, employer or assignee) or any licence holder. The publisher of the work can usually put you in contact with the author, and may even handle your request on the author's behalf. If you want to reproduce not only the content but also the typographical arrangement of the work, you need the publisher's permission as well as that of the author.

When seeking permission, be specific as to *exactly* what material you want to copy or publish, and what you intend to do with it. Always offer full acknowledgement of the author and the work. You are likely to have to pay a fee. The amount will vary according to the material and the use you want to make of it.

The National Standards for Training and Development have, as one of their performance criteria, that 'materials from external sources are adapted and used within the constraints of copyright law'.

There is an alternative, however, to copying materials directly. Remember there is no copyright in ideas. Why not express and develop the ideas yourself (with, to be fair and to avoid plagiarism, proper acknowledgement of the source), and relate them to your organization? This does *not* infringe copyright, provided that you have completely reworked and rephrased the ideas. Even more important, it produces more relevant and therefore more useful material for your learners.

16 Grammar

▷   SUMMARY   ◁

The purpose of grammar is to enable you to communicate your meaning, and grammatical rules are intended to clarify, not mystify. People are often wary about grammar, usually as a result of half-forgotten schoolday maxims. This is unnecessary. Good grammar is merely what communicates correctly.

   However, some points are prone to cause confusion and those are worth considering. This chapter identifies various common parts of speech and grammatical constructions, and then examines some of the trouble spots with:

- Verbs
- Pronouns
- Prepositions
- Adjectives and adverbs
- Phrases and clauses
- Conjunctions

Grammar is Bunk?

Many people, remembering their schooldays, might be tempted to misquote Henry Ford, and maintain that 'Grammar is bunk' and boring bunk at that. It is not. But equally it is not the holy shrine that pedants would make it. Schoolteachers preaching inflexible command-ments, couched in incomprehensible jargon, have a lot to answer for. Grammar is a template, a pattern to help you make your meaning clear to your readers, not iron bonds to constrain you.

   Yes, there are rules, and they are worth following in almost all instances – after all they have a long and honourable pedigree.

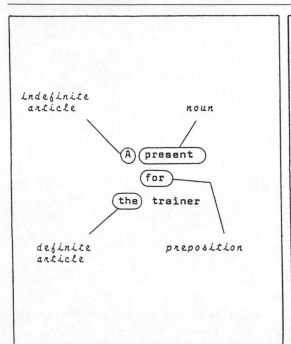

indefinite
article   noun

A present
for
the trainer

definite   preposition
article

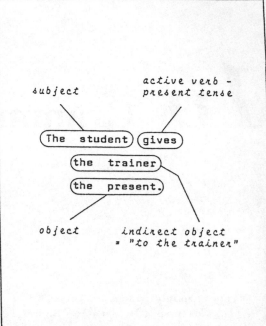

subject   active verb -
               present tense

The student gives
the trainer
the present.

object   indirect object
              = "to the trainer"

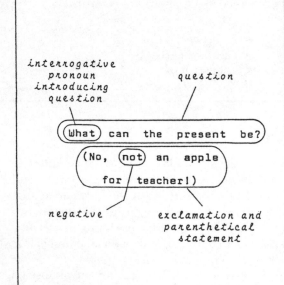

interrogative
pronoun   question
introducing
question

What can the present be?
(No, not an apple
for teacher!)

negative   exclamation and
                parenthetical
                statement

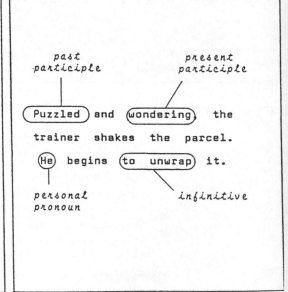

past   present
participle   participle

Puzzled and wondering, the
trainer shakes the parcel.
He begins to unwrap it.

personal   infinitive
pronoun

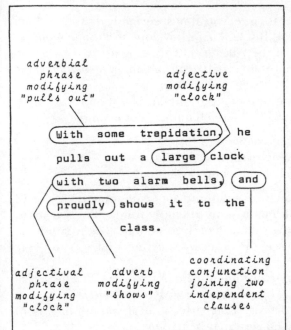

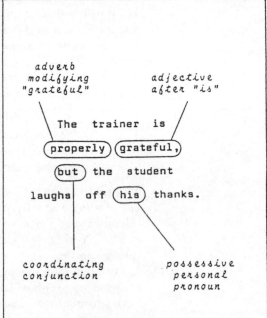

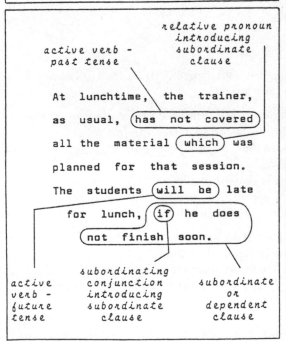

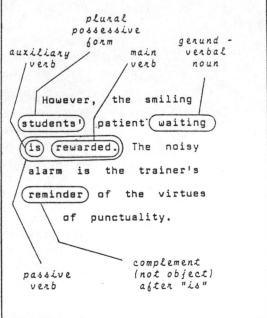

Figure 16.1 *Verbal strip cartoon.*

If English is your mother tongue, you almost certainly do follow them naturally most of the time. But language develops and usage seems to have outstripped some of the rules. Feel free to ignore a rule if you think it will confuse rather than clarify your meaning, *provided that you are sure your reader will not misjudge you and think you ignorant.*

Many people have fixations about grammar, based on those childhood precepts dinned in with a sledgehammer. For example:

– Never split an infinitive.
– Never start a sentence with 'and' or 'but'.
– Never end a sentence with a preposition.

I admit to being rather an un-split infinitive person myself, but even I can understand why you might want to boldly sunder the two parts. The meaning is clear – clearer than 'boldly to sunder ...' or 'to sunder ... boldly'. And, as you can see, the other two maxims I have even fewer qualms about.

Let's examine this grammatical template in more detail. The verbal strip cartoon (Figure 16.1) introduces many of the main parts of speech and grammatical constructions. Refer back to it, if you are unsure of any of the terms mentioned later in this chapter.

Verbs

Some areas of grammar are more prone to cause confusion than others. Verbs are common sinners.

– Splitting, or not splitting, an infinitive I have mentioned above.
– Passives I have also discussed in earlier chapters, eg:
  The trainer was told that ... is not specific and can therefore lead to misunderstanding.
  Student X told the trainer that ... leaves no room for error.
– The subjunctive mood is often used to express hypothetical or impossible conditions. For example:

  If I were you ... (Not: **If I was you** ... since obviously I am not.)
  If the trainer were less long-winded ...
– Many people worry about whether to say 'shall' or 'will'. The grammatical rule is that, for 'I' and 'we', use 'shall' to express an ordinary future tense, and 'will' to express a stronger determination or permission. For 'you', 'he', 'she', 'it', 'they' etc, reverse this – 'will' expresses the plain future and 'shall' determination or permission. For example:

I shall go tomorrow.
I *will* go tomorrow.
The trainer will go tomorrow.
The trainer *shall* go tomorrow.

Americans, however, *always* use 'will' to express the plain future and 'shall' for determination or permission. It does not normally cause any confusion. If in doubt, recast the sentence. For example:

I am determined to go tomorrow.

— Most active verbs are followed by an object on which the verb acts, an object which has, by definition, to be different from the subject of the verb:

The trainer opens the parcel.

However, with the verb 'to be' and a few others (eg 'to seem'), the subject and the following complement (*not* object) refer to the same thing:

The trainer is a pleasant person.

This can cause problems when the complement is a pronoun. We are tempted to use the accusative (object) case, eg **It's me,** rather than the nominative one (subject and complement), eg **It's I. It's me** will not normally cause any misunderstanding, but some people might object to it.

— Having the verb agree with its subject in number (singular or plural) can cause some difficulties. What sounds natural is usually right. Some examples will illustrate:

The students were laughing. Plural subject, so plural verb.
The number of laughing students was large. Singular subject, so singular verb.
A number of the students were laughing. 'A number of' is used as a synonym of 'many', so plural verb.
The class was in agreement. Singular subject, even though it is a collective noun, so singular verb.
The class were disagreeing among themselves. The context makes it clear that the singular noun is being used to mean 'the members of the class as individuals', and so the verb is plural to match.

When two parts of the subject are joined by 'and', the verb is plural:

The student and the trainer were smiling.

When two parts of the subject are joined by 'or' or 'nor', the verb is singular if both are singular. If one or both are plural, make the verb agree with whichever is closer in the sentence:

Either the trainer or the student has left this.
Neither the trainer nor the students have left this.
Neither the students nor the trainer has left this.

'Each' or 'every' is always singular; 'none' may be singular or plural:

Each of the students was filled with anticipation.
There is none so deaf as he who will not hear.
None of the students were going.

– Participles should be clearly attached to the nouns (or pronouns) that they modify. For example, contrast these two:

Having finished their examination papers, the students left.
Having finished their examination papers, the trainer let the students go.

This second example means that the trainer completed the papers; maybe he marked them on the spot. There *is* scope for misunderstanding here.

The same problem arises with the present participle:

After finishing their examination papers ...

– Present participles are very often used instead of gerunds - an easy mistake as they look the same. Participles can be used as adjectives; gerunds are nouns. For example:

The students see the trainer writing on the board. 'Writing' here is a present participle, an adjective modifying 'trainer' – the trainer who is writing.

The students see the trainer's writing on the board. The trainer may not be in the room at all. 'Writing' here is a gerund, a noun, and so has to be preceded by the possessive 'trainer's'. This point, like the last one, may seem pedantic, but again it can cause misunderstanding.

Pronouns

There are various kinds of pronouns – personal, demonstrative ('this', 'that', 'these', 'those'), interrogative ('who', 'which', 'what', 'when', 'how', etc), and relative.

– Personal pronouns, eg **I**, **me**, **him**, **they**, **your**, **its** (note the spelling of **its** and the other possessive forms – no apostrophe), substitute for nouns and cause few problems.

— The biggest area of confusion concerns the relative pronouns **that, what, which, who**. (There are other relative pronouns, eg **when and where,** but their use is fairly straightforward.) Relative pronouns introduce subordinate clauses which relate to a (usually preceding) noun or verb.

'That' restricts the meaning of the preceding noun to 'the particular one':

There is the present that the trainer received. That one and no other.

'Which' and 'who', on the other hand, are non-restrictive pronouns – they merely describe:

The present which the trainer received ...
When using 'who', be careful whether you are relating back to a noun which is a subject or an object (direct or indirect) - an object needs 'whom'. This may sound pedantic, and the incorrect form is unlikely to cause confusion; however it is an error many people notice:

The trainer who received the present ...
The trainer, to whom the student gave the present ...

— Do make clear what a pronoun refers to, or you can easily create ambiguous or even absurd meanings. For example, the famous: **If the baby will not drink raw milk, boil it.** (Even worse is: **If raw milk does not suit the baby, boil it.**)

Prepositions

— Prepositions are linked to nouns or pronouns, eg **to the class, after her.** Usually they precede their objects (the nouns or pronouns), but it is quite acceptable to end a sentence with a preposition, especially if the alternative sounds ridiculously tortuous:

Up to what mischief is the student getting? Up with what tribulations must the trainer put?

— Purists insist that you should not say: **Due to the student's illness, he missed seeing the trainer open the box,** but: **Owing to the student's illness ...**

There is no possibility of misunderstanding, but this is one of

those usages that upset some people. You can, of course, always avoid the problem by writing: **Because the student was ill ...**
– English and American usage often differ over the use of prepositions:

English: **I spoke to Mr Jones yesterday.**
American: **I spoke with Mr Jones yesterday.**

Adjectives and Adverbs

– Adjectives describe (modify) nouns or pronouns.

The curious trainer looked at the clock.
Curious, he looked at the clock.

– Adjectives come in three degrees – positive (eg **curious, happy**), comparative (eg **more curious, happier**), and superlative (eg **most curious, happiest**). The comparative is used to compare two things and is frequently followed by 'than'; the superlative identifies one out of three or more things and is often preceded by 'the':

The trainer was more surprised than the student.
The trainer was the most surprised person in the class.

– Always make comparisons perfectly clear, as they offer scope for misunderstanding:

The trainer appreciated the clock more than the student could mean either: **The trainer appreciated the clock more than the student did** or: **The trainer appreciated the clock more than he appreciated the student.**

– Two comparative adjectives which are often confused are 'less' and 'fewer'. Use 'less' to make a comparative adjective negative (eg **less surprised**) and for quantity, and 'fewer' for number. For example:

The students were less surprised than the trainer.
There was less time than the trainer thought.
There were fewer students than was usual.

– Adverbs modify verbs or adjectives:

Politely the trainer opened the box.
The happily curious trainer opened the box.

— They are often formed by adding '-ly' to an adjective. Their comparative and superlative forms have 'more' and 'most' in front of the adverb:

more politely, most happily.

— It is important that adverbs are in the right place in the sentence otherwise the meaning can change. Contrast these three:

Happily curious as the trainer was, he opened the box.
Curious as the trainer was, he happily opened the box.
Curious as the trainer was, happily he opened the box.
In this last example 'happily' is ambiguous – either it describes the trainer's state of mind, or it can mean 'fortunately'.

Some adverbs need you to pay special attention to placing, eg **almost, only, hardly, wholly, merely.**

Phrases and Clauses

— Phrases are groups of words acting as single grammatical units:

Motivated by politeness (adverbial phrase)**, the trainer opened the box.**
The happily curious trainer (adjectival phrase)**, opened the box.**
Opening the box (noun phrase) **gave the trainer a surprise.**

— The position of phrases in a sentence may sometimes lead to confusion:

The students got permission to take the reports from the trainer.
Did the trainer give the students the permission or the reports or both?

— Clauses must have a main verb and, usually, a subject:
The trainer was surprised, when he opened the box.
The trainer was surprised, and opened the box.

— Phrases and clauses may perform similar grammatical functions:

Motivated also by politeness, the trainer opened the box, which had made him so curious.

It is important, however, not to balance non-parallel forms –

137

this creates a clumsy construction which can distract the reader:

Not: **Motivated by politeness and since he was curious, the trainer opened the box.**

But: **Motivated by politeness and curiosity, the trainer opened the box.**

Not: **To be polite or because he was curious, the trainer opened the box.**

But: **To be polite or satisfy his curiosity, the trainer opened the box.**

Conjunctions

— Clauses, apart from the main clause, are introduced by conjunctions. Subordinating conjunctions (eg **since, when, as**) introduce subordinate or dependent clauses:

Since the trainer was curious, he opened the box.

Coordinating conjunctions (eg **and, but**) introduce coordinate clauses capable of standing independently:

The trainer was curious and he therefore opened the box.

— Coordinating conjunctions are not necessary after semi-colons and colons, but they are permissible and give the second construction more emphasis. For example, contrast:

The trainer was curious; he therefore opened the box.
The trainer was curious; and he therefore opened the box.

The effect is the same if coordinating conjunctions are used at the start of a sentence. For example, contrast:
The trainer was curious. He therefore opened the box.
The trainer was curious. And he therefore opened the box.

Figure 16.2 *Grammar exercise*

Try your hand at some of these. Select the best usage.

1 Which of the two students is (taller / tallest)?
2 Repeating these tests (help / helps) to prove our point.
3 Each of the women must bear (their / her) own responsibility.
4 The Training Committee (has / have) a problem before (them / it).
5 He (has / has considered) and will consider further the student's request.
6 (There / They're / Their) absence was noticed.
7 He asked John, Bob and (I / me) to come.
8 There (was / were) a letter and a memo on the desk.
9 It looks (bad / badly).
10 The person (who / whom / with who / with whom) he met was busy.

Answers

1 **taller** 'Taller' is comparative and 'tallest' is superlative. Use the superlative when referring to three or more.
2 **helps** 'Helps' agrees with the singular subject 'repeating'.
3 **her** 'Her' agrees with the singular pronoun 'each'.
4 **has** and **it** Collective nouns, eg 'committee', take the singular when regarded as a unit.
5 **has considered** You need to insert 'considered', as the two auxiliary verbs 'has' and 'will' take different forms of the main verb. Otherwise the grammatical (non)sense of the sentence is: 'He has consider and will consider further the student's request.'
6 **Their** This is the possessive pronoun. 'There' is the opposite of 'here', and 'they're' the contraction of 'they are'.
7 **me** This is the object of the verb 'asked'. Don't assume that 'I' is always used in a series of names.
8 **were** 'Were' agrees with the plural complement 'letter and memo'.
9 **bad** This is an exception to the rule that verbs are modified by adverbs. Verbs which describe senses, eg 'look', 'feel', 'taste', are modified by adjectives.
10 **whom** The relative pronoun relates to the object of the verb 'met', and so the accusative case 'whom' should be used. 'Meet with' is colloquial, and common in the US, but unnecessary.

17 Punctuation

> SUMMARY <

This chapter considers the DOs and DON'Ts of the main punctuation marks:

- Full stop
- Exclamation mark
- Question mark
- Colon
- Semi-colon
- Comma

- Brackets or parentheses
- Dash
- Hyphen
- Quotation marks
- Apostrophe
- Capitals

Does Punctuation Matter?

Punctuation is often considered the poor relation of the grammar-punctuation-spelling triad, the least important of the three. But punctuation needs as much attention as grammar and spelling – maybe more, as punctuation errors are all too easy to miss in proofreading, and poor punctuation may cause misunderstanding.

The main purpose of punctuation is to make the grammatical construction, and consequently the meaning, of a piece of writing easier for the reader to understand. There have to be rules and conventions, therefore, and the principal ones are outlined in this chapter; however, there is also considerable scope for personal style.

Punctuation does visually what pause and intonation do for speech. Would you deliver a presentation in a non-stop monotone?

Full Stop (.)

DO:
- Use a full stop to end a complete sentence.

The trainer delivered his presentation.

DON'T:
- Break sentences up into ungrammatical fragments by peppering them with unnecessary and incorrect full stops. Eg not:

The trainer delivered. His presentation. Very long. Very verbose. Very boring.
This could, with a certain loss of impact, be one sentence: **The trainer delivered his very long, very verbose and very boring presentation.**
It could also be written as two proper sentences, this time with no loss of impact: **The trainer delivered his presentation. It was very long, very verbose and very boring.**

- Follow all abbreviations with full stops, at least in the UK. In the past it was customary to use full stops after abbreviations but not after contractions (abbreviations which end in the last letter of the word).

Mr, Dr, but **Capt., e.g., etc., p.m.**

But, more and more, full stops are tending to be omitted after **all** abbreviations: **Capt, eg, etc, pm.**

However, full stops following all abbreviations are commonly found in American usage.

Exclamation Mark (!)

DO:
- Use an exclamation mark instead of a full stop to end a genuine exclamation (but not just to add emphasis).

What a presentation the trainer delivered!
- Use it mainly in less formal documents, such as self-learning texts.

DON'T:
- Pepper the text with them. It becomes tedious.

Question Mark (?)

DO:
- Use a question mark instead of a full stop to end a question.

Did the trainer deliver a good presentation?

DON'T:
- Use it to follow an indirect question.

Not: **He asked whether the trainer delivered a good presentation?**
But: **He asked whether the trainer delivered a good presentation.**

Colon (:)

DO:
- Use a colon to introduce a list of items.

The trainer's presentation covered the following points:

- Use it, as an alternative to the comma, to introduce speech.

He asked: 'Did the trainer deliver a good presentation?'

- Use it to join two sentences or coordinate clauses. The colon gives a slightly stronger pause than the semi-colon, and may imply a contrast. It is not as common a usage as the semi-colon.

The trainer delivered his presentation: it was very long, very verbose and very boring.

Semi-colon (;)

DO:
- Consider a semi-colon as a halfway house between a full stop and a comma. It can be used to link complete sentences, where you do not want the break of a full stop and where a comma would be incorrect. In particular, use it to replace a full stop if the second sentence would begin with 'and' or 'but'.

The trainer delivered his presentation; it was very long, very verbose and very boring.
The trainer delivered his presentation as requested; but it was so long, verbose and boring that half his audience fell asleep.

- Use it to separate items in a list.

The trainer's presentation covered techniques for attracting an audience's attention; keeping that attention; persuading an audience; motivating them; and enthralling them.

– *Use* it. The semi-colon is one of the most versatile and under-used of all the stops.

Comma (,)

DO:

– Use a comma to delimit a subordinate clause, a phrase or an adverb at the beginning or end of a sentence. This is not obligatory, but it helps the reader follow the sentence structure, and so grasp the meaning more easily.

Since the trainer was so boring, it was understandable that half his audience fell asleep.
In those circumstances, it was understandable that half the trainer's audience fell asleep.
Understandably, half the trainer's audience fell asleep.

– Similarly, use it to bracket off a subordinate clause, a phrase or an adverb in the middle of a sentence. Again this is not obligatory. Bracketing off adverbs emphasizes them.

It was understandable, since the trainer was so boring, that half his audience fell asleep.
It was understandable, in those circumstances, that half the trainer's audience fell asleep.
Half the trainer's audience, understandably, fell asleep.
Contrast this with:
Half the trainer's audience understandably fell asleep.
This last example places less emphasis on 'understandably' and correspondingly more on 'fell asleep'.

– Use it to separate adjectives qualifying the same noun.

The trainer's presentation was long, verbose and boring.

– Use a comma as a weaker pause than a semi-colon, when you want to join two coordinate clauses where the second begins with 'and' or 'but'.

The trainer delivered his presentation as requested, but it was so long, verbose and boring that half his audience fell asleep.

– Use it as an alternative to the colon to introduce speech.

He asked, 'Did the trainer deliver a good presentation?'

– Use it as an alternative to the semi-colon to separate list items.

The trainer's presentation covered techniques for attracting

143

an audience's attention, keeping that attention, persuading an audience, motivating them, and enthralling them.

The comma before the final 'and' used not to be permissible in the UK. It is now commonly accepted, and can often make the meaning clearer. It is standard in American usage.

DON'T:

— Separate the subject from the verb, however long the sentence seems.

Not: **Techniques for attracting and keeping an audience's attention and persuading, motivating and enthralling an audience, formed the substance of the trainer's presentation.** Omit the comma before 'formed'.

— Use a comma to join two sentences or coordinate clauses *unless* the second begins with 'and' or 'but'. This very common error is called a 'comma fault'.

Not: **The trainer delivered his presentation as requested, it was very long, very verbose and very boring.** Replace the comma after 'requested' with a full stop or semi-colon (or possibly a colon).

— Omit commas delimiting or bracketing off subordinate clauses, phrases or adverbs, where this omission may cause misunderstanding.

Not: **The trainer having finished his audience departed.** At first reading, you may wonder just how lethal the trainer's words were! The clarifying comma solves the mystery. **The trainer having finished, his audience departed.**

Brackets or Parentheses ()

DO:

— Use them, in preference to comma pairs, to bracket off subordinate clauses, phrases or adverbs which are truly parenthetical. They can also bracket off parenthetical sentences or whole passages.

Half the trainer's audience fell asleep (understandably so, given the quality of the presentation). Note that the full stop comes after the closing bracket in English usage, but before it in American.

Contrast this with the next example where the brackets enclose a whole sentence:

Half the trainer's audience fell asleep. (This was understandable given the quality of the presentation.)

Dash (–)

DO:

– Use a single dash in the same way as a colon to introduce lists. Colon dash (:-) is unnecessary.

The trainer's presentation covered the following points –

– Use a single or two dashes as an alternative to commas or brackets.

It was understandable – since the trainer was so boring – that half his audience fell asleep.
Half the trainer's audience fell asleep – understandably so, given the quality of the presentation.

Hyphen (-)

DO:

– Use a hyphen to join linked words where omission could cause misunderstanding.

The trainer was a long standing member of the company suggests that corn plasters may be needed.
The trainer was a long-standing member of the company gives a different message.
Contrast also:
The trainer had blue and red slides.
The trainer had blue-and-red slides.

DON'T:

– If possible use a hyphen to break long words at the end of a line, except at the end of a syllable or between two identical consonants. (NB Unfortuately typesetting of printed materials sometimes infringes this rule.)

thou-sand, mil-lion

– Over-use it.
End of term results is just as easily understood as **End-of-term results.**

145

Quotation Marks (' or ")

DO:

— Be consistent in using single or double quotation marks. You may, however, have to use both if quoting within speech.

The trainer said, 'The manager asked me, "What else could I have done?"'

Apostrophe (')

DO:

— Use an apostrophe to indicate possession. It goes before the additional 's' for singular nouns (and plural ones not ending in 's'), and after the plural 's' for plural nouns. It may go in either place with names ending in 's'.

The trainer's task was finished; so was Mr Jones's. The students' tasks were just beginning.

— Use an apostrophe to indicate the omission of letters in contracted words.

eg let's, don't, it's, I've

DON'T:

— Use it in the possessive form of personal pronouns.

it's means **it is,** not **its.**
they're means **they are,** not **their.**
who's means **who is,** not **whose.**

— Use it to indicate plurals.

Not: **DO's and DON'T's** or **do's and don't's**
But: **DOs and DON'Ts** or **dos and don'ts**

Capitals

DO:

— Use capital first letters for names, place names, titles and, normally, for department and company names.
— Follow your house rules about using capital first letters for other words eg product names.

DON'T:

— Use capital first letters indiscriminately to indicate importance.

Not: **The Company welcomes its Graduates to a new Training Scheme.**

But: **The company welcomes its graduates to a new training scheme.** Note that some house rules insist that 'Company' and often 'Department' are given capital first letters, even though unqualified. Similarly, in contractual writing, defined terms are normally given capital first letters.

Try your hand at punctuating the following passage. You can see my version at the beginning of the chapter, but don't imagine it is the only correct one. There is plenty of room for personal style.

does punctuation matter punctuation is often considered the poor relation of the grammar punctuation spelling triad the least important of the three but punctuation needs as much attention as grammar and spelling maybe more as punctuation errors are all too easy to miss in proofreading and poor punctuation may cause misunderstanding the main purpose of punctuation is to make the grammatical construction and consequently the meaning of a piece of writing easier for the reader to understand there have to be rules and conventions therefore and the principal ones are outlined in this chapter however there is also considerable scope for personal style punctuation does visually what pause and intonation do for speech would you deliver a presentation in a non stop monotone

Figure 17.1 *Punctuation exercise*

18 Spelling

⊳   SUMMARY   ⊲

English spelling consists of a few 'rules' and a lot of exceptions. This chapter considers some common traps:

- ie or ei
- l or ll
- Other single or double consonants in verbs
- -ant or -ent
- -ance or -ence

- -tion or -sion
- -able or -ible
- Plurals
- Negatives
- Abbreviations
- American spellings

The most important spelling rule of all, however, is very simple – if in doubt, consult a dictionary.

Spelling Rules

Grammar and punctuation may allow for personal style: spelling does not. There is usually only one right way to spell a word, although some words are spelt differently in American usage, and some (not all) of these American spellings are acceptable alternatives in the UK.

It is hardly surprising that many people find spelling a problem. There are a handful of spelling rules (we can probably all remember 'i before e except after c') but many exceptions. To complicate matters further, some words are spelt differently according to how they are used. This leads to the inescapable conclusion that the most important spelling rule of all is: look it up in a dictionary. Spelling check programmes on word processors will identify for you any non-existent words you have created (and usually several existing ones too, as their dictionaries are limited), but they will not identify ones which exist but are incorrectly spelt for your meaning (eg **practise/practice**).

But since it would be unbearably tedious to look every word up in a dictionary, it is worth grasping the rules and conventions that do exist.

ie or ei

First of all 'i before e except after c' *only applies to words with an 'ee' sound.* Don't rely on it for words with an open 'eh' sound, eg **leisure, sovereign, their** (although, of course, there is always **friend.**) Examples are:

believe	**ceiling**
chief	**deceive**
fierce	**receive**
niece	

Exceptions are:

counterfeit		⎫ although these are
seize	**either**	⎬ also pronounced
weir	**neither**	⎭ with an 'eye' sound
weird		

l or ll

– Adjectives ending in -l form adverbs ending in -lly.

final	**finally**
general	**generally**

– Adjectives ending in -ll also form their adverbs with -lly endings.

dull	**dully**
full	**fully**

– Adjectives formed by adding -ful (*not* -full) to nouns ending in -ll, lose the second l (in English, but not necessarily in American spelling).

skill	**skilful**

– Verbs ending in single-vowel-plus-l usually double the l in the

149

participles and past tense (in English, but again not necessarily American spelling).

| cancel | cancelled | cancelling |
| travel | travelled | travelling. |

However, note **paralleled** and **parallelled**.

— If the verb ends in double-vowel-plus-l (eg **peel, sail**) or vowel-plus-consonant-plus-l (eg **curl, crawl**) the l stays single, as in **peeled** or **crawling**.

Other Single or Double Consonants in Verbs

b or bb, d or dd, m or mm, n or nn, p or pp, r or rr, s or ss, t or tt.

— When these consonants are found following a single vowel in verbs where the stress is on the last syllable (eg **gas, occur**), they usually double in the participles and past tense of the verb.

ban	banned	banning
gas	gassed	gassing
occur	occurred	occurring
remit	remitted	remitting
stop	stopped	stopping

— Compare verbs where there is a double vowel.

| chain | chained | chaining |
| pair | paired | pairing |

— Compare also verbs where the stress is not on the last syllable.

elicit	elicited	eliciting
limit	limited	limiting
offer	offered	offering
open	opened	opening

— With **bias** and **focus**, also normally follow this pattern (**biased, focused, focusing**) although **biassed, focussed** and **focussing** are sometimes found.

-ant or -ent

There are a few patterns here, but they are not really rules.

- -ate to -ant
  Verbs ending in -ate usually form adjectives and nouns in -ant.
dominate	**dominant**
tolerate	**tolerant**

- -ment
  Nouns with this ending are common (eg **improvement, concealment**). -mant as a noun ending is very rare, but note **informant.**
- -scent
  This ending for adjectives is always -scent, never -scant, as in **acquiescent** and **effervescent**.
- The best source of help really is your dictionary, both for this and the next, allied, problem.

-ance or -ence

- Many -ance or -ence nouns are linked with -ant or -ent adjectives, and so follow the same patterns, few as they are.

dominant	**dominance**	**acquiescent**	**acquiescence**
relevant	**relevance**	**excellent**	**excellence**
tolerant	**tolerance**	**prominent**	**prominence**

- However, there are other -ance and -ence nouns too, where there is no easily distinguishable pattern or guide.

maintenance	**preference**
nuisance	**subsistence**

-tion or -sion

-tion is the more common ending. -sion is found in nouns derived from *some* verbs ending in:

- -end
comprehend	**comprehension**
extend	**extension**
  But note **intend** which gives **intention**.
- -ise
revise	**revision**
supervise	**supervision**

151

— -de

divide	**division**
persuade	**persuasion**

— -rt

convert	**conversion**
divert	**diversion**

But note that **insert** gives **insertion**.

— -ede or -eed

concede	**concession**
succeed	**succession**

— -it

permit	**permission**
transmit	**transmission**

-able or -ible

The question is not only which of these two suffixes you choose, but also whether they alter the spelling of the noun or verb to which they are attached.

In general, -able seems the more common suffix. -ible is often used to create adjectives from the same groups of verbs which gave nouns ending in -sion. (However, these also frequently form adjectives in -ive.)

comprehend	**comprehensible**
convert	**convertible**
divide	**divisible**
permit	**permissible**
supervise	**supervisible**

Once more, I recommend the dictionary. This, obviously, would dispose of the second problem too, but for those of you seeking *general* guidelines on how -able, in particular, affects the spelling of its preceding verbs:

— Verbs ending in -ate often drop this.

demonstrate	**demonstrable**
irritate	**irritable**

– Verbs ending in consonant-plus-e often drop the e.

advise	**advisable**
use	**usable**

– However, verbs ending in -ce and -age keep the e.

enforce	**enforceable**
manage	**manageable**

– Verbs ending in consonant-plus-y change the y to i.

pity	**pitiable**
rely	**reliable**

But, the inevitable exception, **apply** gives **applicable.**

Plurals

Most English nouns form their plurals in -s or -es.

– For nouns ending in consonant-plus-y (but not vowel-plus-y), the y becomes i before adding -es.

sky	**skies**
tray	**trays**

– Some nouns ending in -o add an e before the plural -s; others don't.

potato	**potatoes**
avocado	**avocados**

– Some nouns ending in -f have their plural forms ending in -fs; others claim -ves; still others can take either ending.

proof	**proofs**
knife	**knives**
handkerchief	**handkerchiefs / handkerchieves**

– Nouns ending in -ch, -s, -sh, -ss, or -x normally take -es for their plurals.

box	**boxes**	**splash**	**splashes**
church	**churches**	**summons**	**summonses**
guess	**guesses**		

However some nouns ending in -s, such as **series**, remain unchanged in the plural.

– Nouns ending in -ix normally make their plurals in -ices.

153

> **appendix**   **appendices**
> But **prefix** gives **prefixes.**

- And, to add to the variation, there are also, of course, many totally irregular plurals – the answer remains the same: consult your dictionary.

Negatives

Negative prefixes are added to verbs, nouns, adjectives and adverbs. There is no standard negative prefix.

- Verbs can form their negatives with:

de-	**decipher.**
dis-	**disagree.**
un-	**undo.**

  Negatives beginning with mis- (**misjudge**) imply 'bad' rather than 'not'.

- Nouns can form their negatives with:

de-	**decomposition.**
dis-	**disbelief.**
non-	**non-delivery** (non- is usually hyphenated, but there are exceptions, such as **nonsense**).

  Again, negatives beginning with mis- (**misdemeanour**) imply 'bad'.

- Adjectives, and hence adverbs derived from them, can form their negatives with:

dis-	**dishonest.**	in-	**indecent.**
ig-	**ignoble.**	un-	**unhappy.**

- Adjectives beginning with m- or p- usually form their negatives with im- (**immature, impolite**).
- Adjectives beginning with l- use il- (**illegible**).
- Adjectives beginning with r- similarly use ir- (**irrelevant**).
- Some adjectives have negative forms beginning with non-(hyphenated) (**non-stick**).
- And, as with verbs and nouns, mis- means 'bad' (**misused**), which can be compared to **unused**.

Abbreviations

Some standard abbreviations are often confused and misspelt.

- **cf** means **compare**.
- **etc** means **and others**.
- **eg** means **for example**.
- **ie** means **that is**.
- **NB** means **note**.

American Spellings

No chapter on English spelling would be complete without a comment on American variations. In general, where American spellings differ, they are simpler and more straightforward than English ones.

For instance, words like **practice/practise** and **licence/license** often cause problems. In English, the rule is -ce for the noun and -se for the verb:

> **eg The drinks licence entitles you to sell alcoholic drinks during licensing hours.**

In American spelling, however, -ce serves for both verb and noun.

The main differences between English and American spelling are:

English -our	American -or
colour	**color**
English -ise or -ize	American -ize
rationalise/rationalize	**rationalize**
English -re	American -er
metre	**meter**
English ae and oe diphthongs	American e
haemoglobin	**hemoglobin**
manoeuvre	**maneuver**
English ll in verb forms and some nouns and adjectives	American one l
levelled	**leveled**
traveller	**traveler**
woollen	**woolen**

(But English **skilful** becomes American **skillful**!)

Conclusion

By now, I fear, you may be feeling totally confused and wondering how you ever manage to spell anything correctly. But much of this comes naturally to people for whom English is the first language, and the more widely you read the better your spelling is likely to be. Bad spelling does matter – it gives an unprofessional or careless image to what you write – and it is always avoidable.

I have been stressing the importance of using a dictionary, but some misspellings may become so entrenched in your mind that you are not aware that they are incorrect, and therefore see no need to look them up. Try your hand at the exercise in Figure 18.1 with twenty commonly misspelt words, and remember always to look up any you get wrong!

Which of these forms is correct?

accommodate	acommodate	accomodate
apalled	apauled	appalled
calander	calendar	calender
commemorate	comemorate	commemmorate
committee	commitee	comittee
concensus	consensus	consensous
correspondence	corespondance	correspondance
decisive	dicisive	desisive
delapidated	dilapidated	dillapidated
embarass	embarrass	embarace
fortuitious	fortuitious	fortuitous
homoginious	homogeneous	homogenious
laboratory	laboratary	laborotary
ocurrence	ocurrance	occurrence
parallel	paralell	paralel
recommend	reccommend	recomend
rhinoseros	rhinoscerous	rhinoceros
sutle	suptle	subtle
surreptitious	sureptitious	sureptitous
temporery	temperary	temporary

Answers

accommodate	appalled	calendar	commemorate
committee	consensus	correspondence	decisive
dilapidated	embarrass	fortuitous	homogeneous
laboratory	occurrence	parallel	recommend
rhinoceros	subtle	surreptitious	temporary

Figure 18.1 *Spelling exercise*

19 Tables and Charts

▷ **SUMMARY** ◁

This chapter looks at different ways of presenting numerical information, different chart formats, and the situations most suitable for each. It considers:

- Tables
- Line graphs
- Bar and column charts

- Pie charts
- Organization charts
- Flowcharts
- Decision trees

Tables

There are many ways of presenting numbers, and the way you choose can significantly influence your reader's understanding and interpretation.

The most commonly chosen, although sometimes the least helpful way, is the table.

COURSE PARTICIPANTS 1984 – 1990

	1984	1985	1986	1987	1988	1989	1990	Total
Supervisory Skills – participants	25	20	24	24	10	30	35	168
– dropouts	4	3	4	4	4	2	3	24
Induction – participants	34	38	38	42	30	45	65	292
– dropouts	8	5	6	6	12	10	13	60
Effective Writing – participants	–	–	–	–	–	15	25	40
– dropouts	–	–	–	–	–	2	2	4
Total – participants	59	58	62	66	40	90	125	500
– dropouts	12	8	10	10	16	14	18	88

Figure 19.1 *Table*

Tables have many good points, and others not so good. Among the advantages are:

- They are easy to prepare.
- You can include a lot of information.
- You can compare many variables over two or three dimensions. Here, the dimensions are years and numbers (of participants/ drop-outs), and the different courses are the variables.

The big disadvantages of tables are:

- You can include *too much* information.
- It can be difficult to identify exactly what is important.

Of course, this can be an advantage if you are trying to camouflage any poor results, such as the induction programme's high drop-out level. Figure 19.1 is a horrible table, a jumble of figures thrown together without considering how the reader will use them. Changes in the order, spacing to emphasize the structure of the table or significant aspects, a key or notes explaining particular points, the use of percentages or averages rather than raw numbers – these all aid interpretation. Nor need figures always be precise; often the general impression gained from rounded figures is more important than three places of decimals. Figure 19.2 is more communicative.

COURSE PARTICIPANTS 1985 – 1991

	1985	1986	1987	1988	1989	1990	1991	Ave
Induction – participants	34	38	38	42	30	45	65	42
– dropout % *	19%	12%	14%	13%	29%	18%	17%	17%
Supervisory Skills – participants	25	20	24	24	10	30	35	24
– dropout % *	14%	13%	14%	14%	29%	6%	8%	12%
Effective Writing – participants	–	–	–	–	–	15	25	20
– dropout % *	–	–	–	–	–	12%	7%	9%
Total – participants	59	58	62	66	40	90	125	500
– dropout % *	17%	12%	14%	13%	29%	13%	13%	15%

* % of total nominations

Figure 19.2 *Improved table*

Line Graphs

Figure 19.2 is still not ideal, however. You are trying to compare the size of several variables and this can be better done pictorially. Line graphs used to be unpopular with writers because of the difficulty of preparation, a painstaking, manual task which could not always be delegated to a secretary. The advent of spreadsheet computer packages has made a great difference. These can be linked to word processing packages and use to present raw numbers in various forms, including line graphs.

If you are able to use colour on graphs, you can increase the clarity and even the number of variables. However, colour reproduction is beyond the scope of many trainers for normal use. Nevertheless, by using different line forms (____, ---, ..., __.__.), different point marks (×, *, ○, ●, □, ■, ◇, ◆), or different hatching patterns, you can distinguish up to eight variables quite adequately in black and white (which is probably more than enough for one graph!) Indeed, there is undoubtedly too much information on the graph shown in Figure 19.3, and it would be better to use several short versions covering only the particular variables you want to compare at any point, for instance Induction course and total participants.

Lines on a graph can be zigzag (with straight lines connecting each point) or smoothed out into curves. You can also show a trend line or a 'line of best fit'.

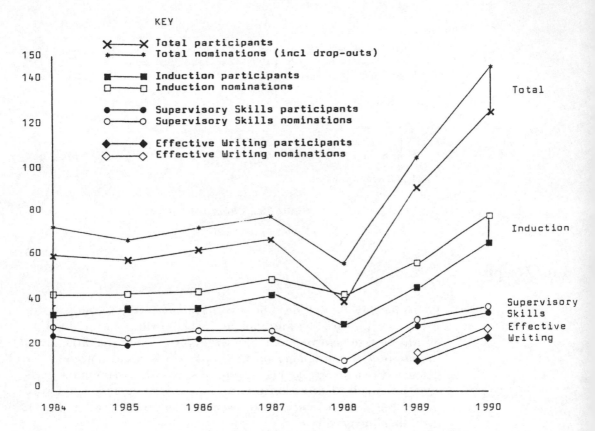

COURSE PARTICIPANTS 1984 – 1990

Figure 19.3 *Line graph*

Note that the line graph can give you a visual appreciation of average values over all variables. In this graph, the averages are obviously somewhere between the levels of the Induction and Supervisory Skills courses. Totals, however, have to be included as a separate set of variables. To make the graph visually stronger, you may want to truncate the space between the totals and the other variables, *but do make it clear that you have done so*, or you risk confusing your reader.

Bar and Column Charts

Bar charts run horizontally across the page, while column charts are vertical. Typically that means that you can have more bars than columns on a chart, but otherwise there is little to choose between these two. They convey less information than tables or graphs, but do give considerable impact.

INDUCTION COURSE PARTICIPANTS 1984 - 1990

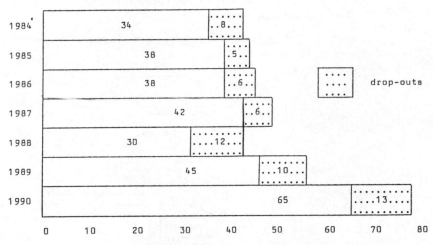

Figure 19.4 *Bar chart*

COURSE PARTICIPANTS 1990

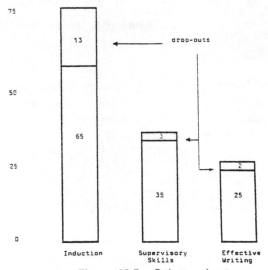

Figure 19.5 *Column chart*

161

Pie Charts

Whereas line graphs and bar and column charts compare size, pie charts show proportion. They are divided into slices which make up the whole, preferably not more than five or six, otherwise labelling each slice becomes awkward without a key. To emphasize one particular slice, cut it out of the pie.

COURSE PARTICIPANTS 1984 - 1990

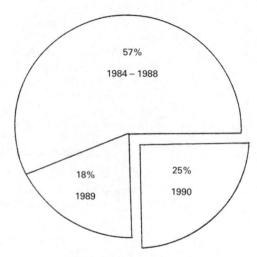

Figure 19.6 *Pie chart*

Organization Charts

These show 'family trees', both of genealogical development and of job reporting structures. Unlike real trees, they 'grow' vertically down from the top, the biggest problem being how to fit in all the 'branches' at one level. Options are:

- Reducing print size as you work down the chart. This has obvious limitations.
- Spreading branches at the same level over two or more lines.
- Switching from horizontal to vertical presentation for the bottom level.
- Removing the development of one or more branches from the main chart and presenting them as separate organization charts.

These last three options have all been shown in the chart below. Do be wary, though, of organization charts as cluttered as this one. Keep information to the necessary minimum by omitting the detail of any branches which are less important for your purpose. Exclude also any details which are likely to change frequently, eg job holders' names – updating organization charts can be time-consuming, and out-of-date charts are positively dangerous.

Obviously, you would not, in one chart, normally use three different ways of dealing with the 'too many branches at one level' problem. The best choice, in this case, would be the last one, with a general organization chart showing the relationship between the departments, and three separate ones for the Information Services, Accounts, and Personnel and Training Departments.

Unbroken lines on organization charts show a direct reporting relationship; broken or dotted lines normally show a secondary or staff relationship. These can easily over-complicate a chart, however, so unless they are really necessary, avoid them and simply mention the secondary relationship as a footnote.

MANAGEMENT SERVICES DIVISION

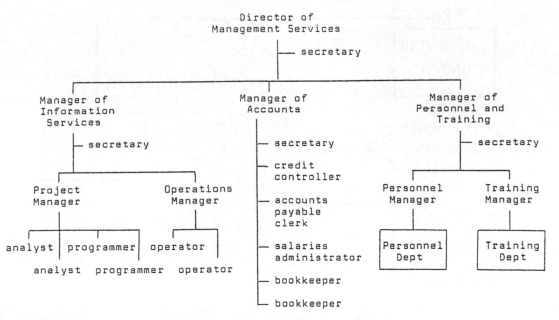

Figure 19.7 *Organization chart*

Flowcharts

These show the progression of an activity. Common in Information Services applications, they are also extremely useful for other areas. In particular, they can be an excellent alternative to lengthy procedures and job aids. There are many standard flowchart symbols and, although some of these may not be relevant to training applications, the more common ones are worth learning and using correctly. Drawing templates of the various symbols eases the drafting chore.

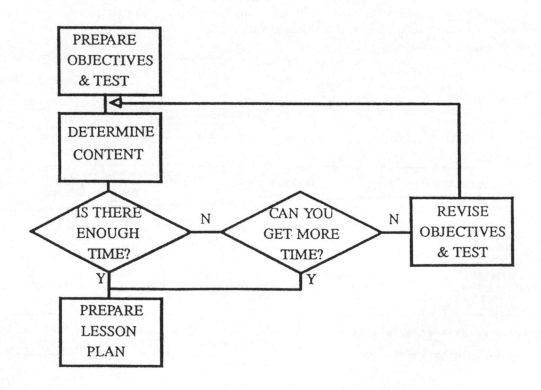

Figure 19.8 *Flowchart*

Decision Trees

To look at, these resemble organization charts although, equally unnaturally, they often grow from left to right. In function, they combine the organization chart's representation of dependent relationships and the flowchart's progress picture. They identify the different options available at any point, their likely outcomes, and any consequent options for each of the outcomes etc. Maze exercises can all be plotted as decision trees. However, their greatest use is as decision-making tools, where they can be combined with numerical weightings.

The decision tree in Figure 19.9 examines the options for a negotiation skills course. Each of the options is divided into different possible outcomes with their presumed likelihood and costs/benefits. These could be used to calculate an overall 'best' choice.

Clearly, a decision tree can easily get very complicated. As with organization charts, it is often helpful to present a simplified global chart, with each of the branches developed as sub-charts.

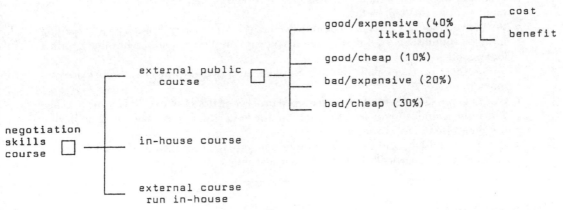

Figure 19.9 *Decision tree*

20 Using Technology

$\triangleright$ SUMMARY $\triangleleft$

This chapter considers various technological aids the trainer/writer may want to use, and the opportunities they offer.

- Dictating machines, although hardly new technology, can be extremely helpful, but many people use them badly.
- Word processors are an enormous improvement on typewriters. Editing is easy; spelling mistakes diminish, even if they do not disappear completely; and the finished product looks good.
- Spreadsheet packages allow you to manipulate and present numerical information in many ways.
- Graphics packages do for design what word processing does for text. This is one package which the trainer should aim to master – in the long run, it is much easier than having someone else interpret your ideas.
- Desktop publishing pulls text and graphics together to produce professional-looking documents. It is particularly useful for self-learning texts.

Dictating Machines

They may have been around for a long time, but many people misuse them and others refuse to use them at all. This is a pity as they can save a lot of time. For you, it is quicker to speak than to write, and for your secretary, to type without having to read (and decipher!) a handwritten draft.

One reason people do not use them is that they are embarrassed by the sound of their voice. Trainers should not find this a problem – if

166

you don't know what you sound like by now ... The answer, anyway, is practice. Soon you will no longer hear the voice but only the words.

A second problem may be that you have tried using a dictating machine, but found that you dried up – the words did not come easily, or even at all. The answer, again, is practice and preparation.

Dictated drafts need to be planned as carefully as handwritten ones. At the very least, before you begin you should:

- Know your objective, what you want to achieve.
- Identify all the points you want to make.
- Sequence them.
- Have all reference material, previous correspondence etc to hand.

A few simple tips can improve your dictation enormously.

- Give your secretary any background information or instructions *at the beginning*. The best way to lose a secretary is to say, at the end of a long letter, 'By the way, please type this on plain and not headed paper.' (Unless, that is, she is using a word processor, but even then the principle is a good one.)
- If giving instructions within the document, precede them with your secretary's name as an alert signal.
- Decide with your secretary what, if any, punctuation you will give. You should, in any case, indicate when you want to start a new paragraph.
- Speak in natural phrasing, with short pauses for commas and longer ones for full stops.
- Spell all names and any difficult words.
- *Practise* until you are familiar with the equipment.

Dictating machines are more helpful with some documents than with others. You may need to *see* the draft of a long, complex report as you write it, in order to refer back to earlier sections. On the other hand, dictating machines are ideal for lesson plans (they keep you thinking in *spoken* language), and for letters and memos. After all, could you, without wanting to burst out laughing, hear yourself actually saying: 'Pursuant to our previous correspondence, wherein, as may easily be ascertained, lies a systematic exposition of the fundamental principles of ...'?

Word Processors

A word processing package stores typed text on a computer, so that it can be copied, searched and edited freely. This has revolutionized the production of written materials.

The most important point, for the writer, is that you can edit properly without being constrained by the thought: 'Dare I insert this paragraph on page 1, and so force my secretary to retype the next six pages too?' With a word processor, you have total freedom to change what you have written, to move a passage from one part of the document to another, or to alter your layout completely.

Of course, that is no reason for giving your secretary scrappy or ill-prepared first drafts. However it *is* often easier to judge how a document reads once it is typed, and in reality word processing drafts are, and should be, submitted at an earlier stage than those for typewriter production.

Word processors also offer a variety of useful language aids. The one most commonly found is a spelling check. As I have pointed out in other chapters, *this does not guarantee that all the words in the document are correctly spelt.* What the spelling check does is compare each word with the word processor's inbuilt dictionary. If a word is 'not found', you can correct your spelling or add your word to the dictionary. However the spelling check will not pick up 'we' (when you meant 'wet') or 'peace' (for 'piece'). Incidentally, most spelling checks give you a word count, which can be useful.

Other language aids which you may find are:

- A Thesaurus, giving you words of similar meaning.
- A grammar check. Similar to the spelling check, this checks your sentence structure and punctuation against preset rules and formats. Sometimes these may seem rather archaic, depending on the type of document you are writing. You can, if you wish, ignore the suggested corrections.
- A style check. These are not normally included as standard in word processing packages but are available separately, often combined with a grammar check. They tend to perform the equivalent of a FOG Index, concentrating on sentence and word length, and also the use of passive verbs. Some style checks offer suggested alternative versions.

A further word processing facility, which can be helpful with long documents, is contents listing and indexing. This is achieved by searching the document for key words.

Most trainers will get their drafts word processed by a secretary. However, if you can use a word processor yourself, you can make your amendments without having to have the document printed first. You do not need to be a fluent typist to achieve this. Two- or four-finger typing is quite adequate, and the word processing packages themselves are very easy to understand and use ('user-friendly' in the jargon). Making your own corrections is even more straightforward in companies with electronic mail systems – you read in the draft your secretary has prepared, edit it, and send or print it yourself.

But what about those of us who freeze at the sight of a computer screen and keyboard? It is worth overcoming this reluctance with *private* practice. It is virtually impossible to wreck any modern computer system, and most user manuals are now very simply and clearly expressed. They also include basic tuition packages designed to give the tyro the skill and confidence to experiment further. Remember, it is not necessary to be a trained typist.

Spreadsheet Packages

These are designed to allow you to store, retrieve, calculate and display large quantities of numerical information. The standard display format is a tabular one, but most spreadsheet packages will also present the information as a line graph, a bar or column chart, or a pie chart. The sizes of the bars, columns and pie slices, and the exact slope of the graph lines are calculated for you by the package.

Many word processing and spreadsheet packages can be linked so that spreadsheet information can be incorporated into a word processing document.

Graphics Packages

Even if you do not feel it worthwhile to become expert with a word processor or spreadsheet package, learning to use a graphics package will transform your visuals. Graphics packages help you to produce attractive and professional-looking charts, graphs, drawings and course visuals.

Let's take a look at a few examples. In Chapter 19, I suggested that pie charts are an excellent way of showing proportions. Compare the simple pie chart, produced manually, with the one produced by the graphics package.

COURSE PARTICIPANTS 1985-1991

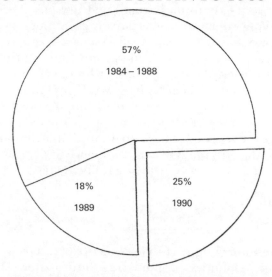

COURSE PARTICIPANTS 1984-1990

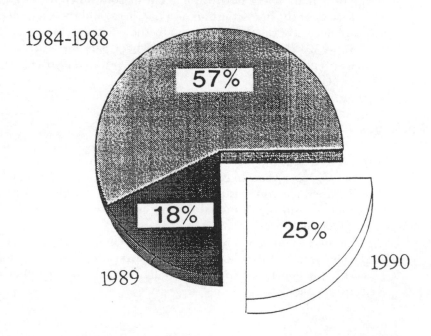

Figure 20.1 *Hand-drawn and graphics package pie chart*

Similarly, in Chapter 9, I suggested that stick men are perfectly adequate in cartoon drawings. So they are, but a graphics package will offer you a range of super-stick men.

Figure 20.2   *Hand-drawn and graphics package cartoon*

Graphics packages offer a variety of lettering styles and sizes for headings and text, and a gallery of ready-drawn shapes and pictures for you to choose from. You can also draw your own pictures straight on to the computer screen. (You normally use a hand-held gadget called a 'mouse', as this is easier than a keyboard.) You can sometimes also scan in pictures or even photographs using an electronic scanner.

Among the visual effects which can be produced by most packages are:

- 3D charts
- Drop shadows (a shadow below and beside the drawing, letter or symbol) to give emphasis.
- Variable shading, of a gradual, regularly increasing or decreasing intensity.

You may also be able to use a wide range of colours (often up to 60 or more shades), although this depends on the capability of your printer or slide maker. Most graphics packages will produce 35mm slides or overhead transparencies, provided you have the appropriate output device.

Although graphics packages are fairly complicated, it is worth learning to use one yourself. Otherwise you are dependent on somebody else's interpretation of your ideas, which, with such an enormous range of options available, may be very different from what you intended.

Desktop Publishing

Word processed text looks attractive but ordinary. You can enhance the appearance by good layout and illustrations, but the effect is workmanlike and efficient rather than smoothly impressive. Where presentation is critical, you can improve on word processing by using a desktop publishing package.

What might you use it for? The most obvious application would be self-learning texts, but it is also invaluable for forms and questionnaires.

To see what a desktop publishing package can achieve, consider the sample pages from a self-learning text, which I used as an illustration in Chapter 12. They were created with typed text (photo-reduced where necessary) and hand-drawn illustrations, physically cut-and-pasted to make up the page. The result, I would suggest, is perfectly adequate for in-house training materials. It is not, however, as professional looking or as inviting to use as the desktop publishing version.

Desktop publishing combines text and graphics – the text may be ready word processed and the graphics prepared using a graphics package, or they may both be created using the desktop publishing package itself.

Significant features are:

- Various styles and sizes of lettering can be used.
- Text can be laid out in several columns and, if desired, justified. (The spaces between the words are expanded or contracted so that each line of text fills the complete width of the column.)
- Text can flow round the graphics, enclosing their shape.
- A variety of colours is available, depending on the capabilities of your printer.

See
also

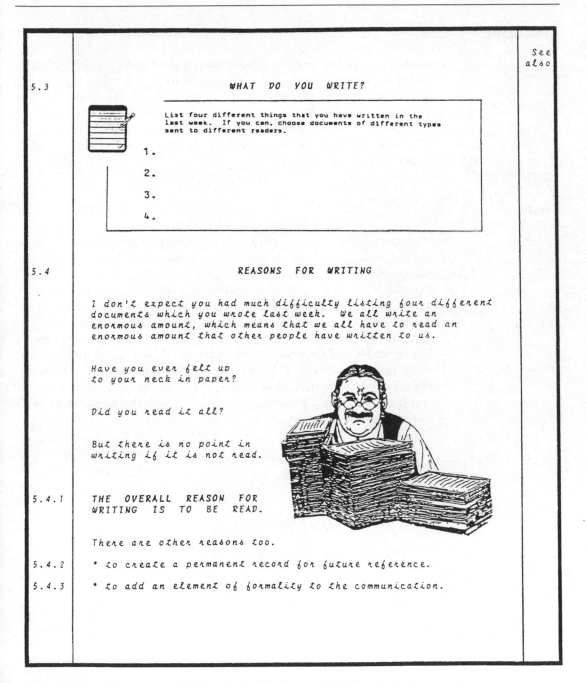

5.3
WHAT DO YOU WRITE?

List four different things that you have written in the last week. If you can, choose documents of different types sent to different readers.

1.

2.

3.

4.

5.4
REASONS FOR WRITING

I don't expect you had much difficulty listing four different documents which you wrote last week. We all write an enormous amount, which means that we all have to read an enormous amount that other people have written to us.

Have you ever felt up to your neck in paper?

Did you read it all?

But there is no point in writing if it is not read.

5.4.1
THE OVERALL REASON FOR WRITING IS TO BE READ.

There are other reasons too.

5.4.2
* to create a permanent record for future reference.

5.4.3
* to add an element of formality to the communication.

Figure 20.3 *Desktop publishing page*

Authoring Systems

Authoring systems enable you to design your own computer-based instructional programmes. I mention them only because they are a technological product aimed specifically at trainers. However, I do not intend to discuss them in any detail, as computer-based materials are outside the scope of this book. Most authoring systems also require a fair level of technical knowledge, and are therefore less likely to be of general interest to trainers.

Costs

You may wonder if some of these facilities are beyond the scope of your training budget. Costs depend on whether you have to buy the equipment or just the computer software. Equipment is still fairly expensive, but it is actually dropping in price as the demand grows. Word processors and PC's (personal computers) are very reasonably priced for the capacity they offer. More specialized equipment, such as slide makers or digital scanners, are comparatively more expensive, but, as with word processors, prices are likely to drop as they become more commonly used. The same is true for the software. The more commonly used it is, the cheaper it becomes. In general, the cost of computer software compares favourably with other training costs, such as outside courses or videos.

Appendix 1
Further Reading

Writing

G.V. Carey, *Mind the Stop*, Penguin Books, 1976
Chambers Concise Dictionary, Chambers, 1990
The Concise Oxford English Dictionary, Oxford University Press, 1990
Geoffrey Crabb, *Copyright Clearance: a Practical Guide*, National Council for Educational, Technology, 1990
Sir Ernest Gowers, rev Sidney Greenbaum and Janet Whitcut, *The Complete Plain Words*, Penguin Books, 1986
H. Hart, *Hart's Rules for Compositors and Readers*, Oxford University Press, 1983
Darrell Huff, *How to Lie with Statistics*, Penguin Books, 1973
J.E. Metcalfe, *The Right Way to Spell*, Elliott Right Way Books, 1980
Eric Partridge, *Usage and Abusage*, Penguin Books, 1973
Roget's Thesaurus, Penguin Books, 1987
A.J. Thomson and A.V. Martinet, *Oxford Pocket English Grammar*, Oxford University Press, 1990
Tom Vernon, *Gobbledegook* National Consumer Council, 1980

Training Materials

Business, Commerce and Industry, Dynamic Graphics, Inc, 1980
Colin Corder, *Teaching Hard, Teaching Soft*, Gower, 1990
Jackie Elton, *Letter Writing*, Industrial Society, 1988
Antony Jay, *Slide Rules*, Video Arts, 1976
Robert Mager, *Preparing Instructional Objectives*, Kogan Page, 1990

National Standards for Training and Development, Training and Development Lead Body, 1991

Phil Race, *The Open Learning Handbook*, Kogan Page, 1989

ed Michael Stevens, *Case Studies*, BACIE, 1990

Bernard Ungerson, *How to Write a Job Description*, Institute of Personnel Management, 1983

Judith Vidal-Hall, *Report Writing*, Industrial Society, 1988

Appendix 2
Information Services

British Association for Commercial and Industrial Education (BACIE), 16 Park Crescent, London W1N 4AP

British Institute of Management, Management House, Cottingham Road, Corby, Northants NN17 1TT

Confederation of British Industry, Quadrant Court, 49 Calthorpe Road, Edgbaston, Birmingham B15 1HT

Industrial Society, 48 Bryanston Square, London W1H 7LN

Institute of Personnel Management, IPM House, Camp Road, Wimbledon, London SW19 4UW

Institute of Training and Development, Marlow House, Institute Road, Marlow, Bucks SL7 1BN

National Council for Educational Technology, 3 Devonshire Street, London W1N 2BA

Plain English Campaign, 15 Canal Street, Whaley Bridge, Stockport SK12 7LS

Training and Development Lead Body, The Employment Department, Qualifications and Standards Branch (QS7), Room E704, Moorfoot, Sheffield S1 4PQ